PICTORIAL GUIDE TO

Silvered Mercury Glass

IDENTIFICATION & VALUES

Diane Lytwyn

COLLECTOR BOOKS

A Division of Schroeder Publishing Co., Inc.

Front cover:
Vase, made in Bohemia, 12" tall, nineteenth century, $950.00.
Back cover:
Left to right: Vase (one of a pair), made in England, 1849 – 1855, 9" tall, cased green glass cut to silver, signed E. Varnish & Co., London, $8,000.00 ($16,000.00 the pair). Goblet, made in England, 1849 – 1855, 9" tall, cased blue glass cut to silver, signed E. Varnish & Co., London. $6,000.00. Goblet, made in Bohemia, 1860 – 1880, 6" tall, ruby red flashing cut to silver, $675.00.

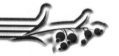

Cover design by Beth Summers
Book design by Lisa Henderson
All photographs by author Diane C. Lytwyn

COLLECTOR BOOKS
P.O. Box 3009
Paducah, Kentucky 42002-3009

www.collectorbooks.com

Copyright © 2006 Diane Lytwyn

The current values in this book should be used only as a guide. They are not intended to set prices, which vary from one section of the country to another. Auction prices as well as dealer prices vary greatly and are affected by condition as well as demand. Neither the author nor the publisher assumes responsibility for any losses that might be incurred as a result of consulting this guide.

Searching For A Publisher?

We are always looking for people knowledgeable within their fields. If you feel that there is a real need for a book on your collectible subject and have a large comprehensive collection, contact Collector Books.

Contents

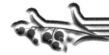

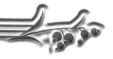

Foreword

In 2001, the Museum of American Glass at Wheaton Village in Millville, New Jersey, organized an exhibition titled "Mirror Images: American Silvered Glass." This ground-breaking exhibit presented the story of American silvered glass. Objects were borrowed from Diane Lytwyn, other private collectors, and from institutional collections, including the Corning Museum of Glass, the Sandwich Glass Museum, The Jones Museum of Glass and Ceramics, and the Historical Society of Western Pennsylvania. A catalog accompanied the show and was the first publication ever written solely about American silvered glass. The idea for this exhibition actually came from Diane Lytwyn.

Several years before, Diane had visited our museum and made a point of contacting me about our small display case of silvered glass. Wanting to see quality silvered glass in American museums, she generously lent pieces from her personal collection, revitalizing our exhibit. She also spent the time to educate me about the refined beauty of American silvered glass and to teach me the differences found in American pieces, which set them apart from English and European examples.

Serious collectors, like Diane Lytwyn, help museums by sharing their knowledge and their collections. Diane definitely made an impact on the Museum of American Glass and me, personally. There would not have been an exhibition without her inspiration. Over the years, I have admired her vast knowledge on the subject of silvered glass and I know she will bring her wealth of information to this publication.

Gay LeCleire Taylor
Curator/Director
Museum of American Glass

Dedication

This book is dedicated to my husband, Paul, who shares a love of mercury silvered glass and who encouraged me to write this book. Without his support, patience, and understanding, this work would have never been written.

I would also like to dedicate this book to the memory of the late Blanche Hallquist, who owned the antique shop in Stratford, Connecticut. It was because of Blanche that I became interested in this beautiful glass, and I will always remember her kindness.

Preface

Silvered glass, also known as mercury glass, was patented in England, Germany, and the United States, and was made by many companies beginning around the middle of the nineteenth century. In spite of its significant production, which lasted from about 1850 to 1930, there is much confusion about the origin and history of this unusual glass.

My interest in this unique ware began in 1973, when a chance visit to an upscale antiques shop in New Haven, Connecticut, piqued my interest in the subject of decorative glass. I was dazzled by the array of art glass on display, but felt naïve because I knew nothing about any of the lustrous and colorful glass pieces labeled "Tiffany" and "Steuben." Determined to learn more about the subject of glass, and antiques in general, I bought a copy of Kovel's *Know Your Antiques* and read it from cover to cover. Since I was already interested in glass, I focused much of my attention on that particular chapter, and can recall the exact moment when I saw an American mercury glass master salt in one photograph. For me, this intriguing object was one of the most exquisite things I had ever seen, so sleek, shiny, and silvery, yet made of glass!

Some months later, while browsing in a small antiques shop in Stratford, Connecticut, I spotted a shiny, silvery object in the back of an old oak curio cabinet and knew immediately it was a piece of mercury glass. I remember feeling proud of being able to identify the piece, and was very happy that the shop owner, an elegant and kindly woman, seemed to share my enthusiasm for this discovery. From that moment on, I began to search for more pieces of the rare and mysterious glass that has truly become a collecting focus and lifetime source of study.

Although my ability to find other pieces of mercury glass satisfied the acquisition need, my quest for further information on the subject was very frustrating. I soon discovered that many books on antiques, even those devoted exclusively to glass, often contained little, if any, information about mercury glass. Except for a few notable publications, mercury glass was actually ignored. I began to wonder how and why it could have been missed, since this unusual glassware is so remarkable in its distinction from other types of glass.

Adding to my frustration was the fact that even when I did discover a passage or paragraph about silvered mercury glass, statements were often conflicted, and descriptions were usually inaccurate, as compared to the pieces in my growing collection. Were it not for the notable publications by Kenneth Wilson and Albert Christian Revi, whose books *New England Glass and Glassmaking* and *Nineteenth Century Glass: It's Genesis and Development*, I would have not had any information. Those two authors, unknown to each of them, had become my virtual partners, for at least they seemed to know and appreciate this unusual ware!

Determined to find out more about mercury glass, I traveled to a United States Patent Office branch to examine descriptions of nineteenth century patents on microfiche, searched through old advertising, catalogs, and trade-cards, and visited many museums to view their collections and research pertinent archival materials.

As I continued to collect silvered glass, I began to notice the differences in weight, decoration, style, form, and quality, and finally realized that the best source of study came from the glass itself. I came to understand that a thoughtful examination of the differences or similarities in the sealing methods, forms, and design techniques inherent in each piece could offer important clues regarding both authentication and attribution. By treating each silvered mercury glass item as a unique specimen for study, it is possible to gain much information about the age, origin, and maker of the object.

The premise of this book, therefore, is to provide piece-by-piece pictorial evidence accompanied by detailed and item-specific notations, which will help the reader learn visually about this unusual art glass. Each illustration is accompanied by an approximate current value, which is intended only as a guide, rather than a fixed price. Values vary greatly, depending on the rarity, condition, and demand by collectors, and are supported both by final auction results as well as current retail sales prices for 2005.

Introduction

Is It Silvered Or Mercury Glass?

Silvered glass, commonly known as mercury glass, describes glass that was made double walled, then silvered between the layers with a liquid silvering solution, and sealed. Most of this glass was free blown, although molds were used to create some forms. Although the use of the term "mercury glass" is a misnomer because mercury was never used in the formula for silvering tableware and vases, the term itself has become synonymous with silvered glass products. Some authors have attempted to distinguish "silvered glass" from "mercury glass," often treating the glass as two distinct subjects. The criteria cited for this distinction is often vague and nebulous. While some authors refer to the cased and layered English examples as "silvered glass," still others label the American pieces as "mercury glass." However, the English makers crafted plain mirror pieces, and several companies in the United States made plated or cased items, which has resulted in much confusion about the proper name for this interesting glass. Although elemental mercury was likely not a part of the formula used to silver the pieces in this book, nearly every one of the objects illustrated in the following chapters was described as "mercury glass" at the time of acquisition.

Research for the first written use of that particular moniker revealed some important facts. The term "mercury glass," was found in the monumental work *American Glass*, published in 1941 and written by George and Helen McKearin, who were noted authorities on the subject. The Chronological Chart of American Glass Houses, in *American Glass*, contains information describing the products of the Boston Silver Glass Company as: "flint and silver (mercury) glass." Prior to the book's publication, and in an article titled "Glass at World's Fairs," for the August 1939 edition of the magazine *Antiques*, Helen McKearnin references English glass exhibited at the 1851 Crystal Palace Exposition and states: "The other, of 'glass silvered by Hale Thompson's (sic) process, a recent development in glassmaking,' was apparently of the type of glass we call mercury."

This would seem to support the contention that "mercury glass," therefore, was the common expression used for silvered glass, even by authors of such renown.

In an article written by glass historian Lura Woodside Watkins, titled "American Silvered Glass," published in the October 1942 issue of the magazine *Antiques*, the dilemma is first explored:

"Variously known as silver glass, mercury glass, or silvered glass...bewilderment concerning the ware is reflected in the lack of a uniform cognomen for it. The preferable, and indeed only correct appellation is silvered glass, for this ware is a clear metal to which a silvery lining has been applied. The term silver glass incorrectly implies the use of silver substance in the composition of the glass itself. The expression mercury glass was common many years ago and is still heard today; it derives from the belief that the glass was coated like a mirror with mercury backing. Mercury, however, was rarely used to produce a silver effect, and never on tableware. It is true that the Boston Silver Glass Company used the popular misnomer, which, as it is certainly easier to say, may eventually be adopted by collectors. The contemporary term used by glassmakers was silvered."

In fact, Watkins's prediction became a reality, and while subsequent articles referred to the glass as "silvered," the term "mercury glass" has become colloquial for silvered glass. Rather than debate the issue further, I have decided to include both, as my contributions focus on the intricate art of the glass itself, and not on the nuances of semantics. It should be noted, however, that most scholars refer to the glass as "silvered" and pieces displayed in museums are rarely "mercury." In fact, the glass was always described as "silvered glass" in manufacturing catalogs, on trade cards, and in virtually all written references describing the ware from its origin in the nineteenth century.

Perhaps the recent commercial use of the term "mercury glass" to label and market brand new, mass-produced household goods, including Christmas ornaments, would tend to tarnish the term. The truth remains, however, that the average person will recognize the name "mercury glass" far more often than the term "silvered glass."

Curiously enough, English-speaking people are not alone with regard to the appropriate term for this glassware. For people that speak German, the term "Bauernsilber," which translates roughly to "farmer's silver," is used most commonly to describe "Silberglas," which is "silvered glass." Another term used is "peasant silver" which may have evolved because of the perception that silvered glass was a less expensive substitute for solid silver.

While many authors agree that an obvious correlation exists between the appearance of double-walled silvered glass and their counterpart objects formed of the metal silver, people acquired these objects for their inherent value as decorative glass, and not as a substitute for silver. The prevailing styles of nineteenth century sterling silver forms were in no way comparable to silvered glass pieces.

In fact, the evolution of blown silvered glass during the mid-nineteenth century, which included the use of engraved grapevine, floral and leaf designs originating in Bohemia, as well as the festoons, garlands wreaths, and other neoclassical motifs from the Anglo-Irish tradition, were concurrent to most blown glass of the same period.

A profusion of decorating techniques, as well as the development of other intricate patterns that were influenced by Byzantine and Far Eastern traditions, greatly affected the emerging design lexicon of silvered glass. Silvered glass was, therefore, "glass" first and foremost.

The initial appearance of this remarkable ware caused a great sensation, and it quickly gained favor among Victorian-era patrons both here and abroad. Although speculative, the success of silvered glass may have occurred because of its shiny and glittering appeal, as it certainly was a stunning departure from the aesthetic tedium of the clear glass items produced in the first decades of the nineteenth century.

Often described incorrectly as a "novelty," the production of silvered glass was neither short-lived nor incidental, for its production lasted for over 60 years. Silvered glass continues to enjoy great admiration today, as evidenced by its status as a highly sought collectible antique art glass.

The silvering of glass for ornamental purposes may have originated as early as the late seventeenth century, but the decorative accessories and tableware, known today as mercury glass, were made from the middle of the nineteenth century and continued into the twentieth century.

Demanding immediate visual attention, these sparkling glass marvels have surprised and delighted observers for over 150 years. Silvered glass first appeared as whimsy when experimental, often mysterious liquid materials were used to provide a reflective surface to the interior of soda lime glass spheres blown in a single layer. These "watch balls" were hung surreptitiously near doorways, possibly as a surveillance measure, for their reflective qualities enhanced the ability to monitor entrances. Subsequently, some superstitious owners came to view the globes as protection against evil spirits, based on the premise that a witch could not tolerate her own reflection, and the spheres became known as "witch-balls." Whether based on truth or simply a myth, these legends provide great romance to the story of silvered glass.

Each country has its own unique history concerning the development, design, and evolution of silvered mercury glass.

In general, the lack of patent or design protection and the rise of glass experimentation conducted in the nineteenth

century appeared to support the almost simultaneous appearance of this artistic glassware in Bohemia, Germany, England, and the United States, although the span of production years often varied. The stylistic influences of the continental Bohemian and German artisans are evident in many engraved examples made in America, while the use of colored glass layers perfected in England impacted the fabrication of the glass made by makers in the United States. Simply stated, glass workers often copied or imitated each other, and the immigration patterns of the third quarter nineteenth century contributed towards a growing Continental influence in America's developing glass industry. Evidence of an interchange of construction methods, as well as design techniques, is obvious in many of the articles produced in different countries.

One speculation, made by authors who have investigated the methods of creating silvered glass, is that the important step used in the blowing of double-walled vessels involved the inversion of the molten glass bubble back into the interior of the piece. This maneuver was necessary in order to form the two layers into which the silvering solution was introduced. However, sealing methods, which often provide the most important clue in the determination of origin, vary greatly from country to country, and even maker to maker.

The following sections will provide information about the production, designs, and sealing methods of silvered glass, which appertain to each country.

Rudimentary forms of glass subjugated to early methods of silvering first appeared in the second to third decade of the nineteenth century in the areas around Haida, Bohemia.

Bohemia, now the Czech Republic, long considered an important source for glass manufacturing in general, includes areas of Austria, Germany, and Poland. The manufacture of silvered glass, or silberglas, appeared to evolve first from about 1840, where molded glass statuary, often depicting Christ or the Madonna and Child, were created for religious use in rural areas. In addition, candlesticks, or "Kerzenleuchter," were fairly common, as well as beakers, footed beakers, and vases purchased by the general population, and made for export.

One of the first clues in determining the place of origin is to understand that Bohemian, German, and Continental silvered glass was made, generally, from glass that did not contain lead.

In order to determine silvered glass by origin, it is necessary to understand the basic chemistry of glass itself. Glass is an amorphous material comprised of different substances. There are several ingredients that compose the formula for most glass, which are silica, or sand; sodium carbonate, or soda; and potassium carbonate, or potash. The proportions and additions of other materials in the formula have a direct effect on the melting point, strength, clarity, and weight of the finished glass. Thus, the strength and weight of the glass became an important consideration regarding the decorative techniques that could be used. Most non-lead glass, for example, would not endure the pressure of the cutting wheel, and therefore, the vast majority of Bohemian and German silvered glass items were decorated by other methods.

It must be noted that the development of Bohemian "crystal," which included alkali in the form of lime, often produced a metal or glass batch that was strong enough to sustain surface wheel engraving. However, since the glass was blown into thin double walls, true wheel engraving is rare to find in Bohemian silvered glass.

It is probably because of this fact that the glass artisans of Bohemia developed an astonishing array of decorating techniques for silvered glass, which often serve to distinguish their wares from others.

In addition to the method of surface painting, other techniques included glass powder granulate application, acid etching, acid-vapor satin matting, beading, cold enamel work, flashing, staining, and even the application of glass "jewels." In addition to providing the most diverse methodology for surface decorating, the glassmakers of Bohemia were also the most prolific in terms of sheer production. According to one comprehensive source exploring the glass industry in Bohemia around 1874, one firm alone employed 200 workers specifically for the production of silvered glass.

There is also speculation that a certain amount of silvered glass may have been decorated by artisans paid at home by the piece, thus creating a new cottage industry in Bohemia and Germany.

Regardless of the specific origin in Bohemia, Germany, or later, Czechoslovakia, silvered mercury glass enjoyed great popularity and was produced well into the twentieth century. The silvered glass products of

Bohemia and Germany often vary in quality, and examples can be found with naïve, and even crude painting, or with decorative embellishments that are truly outstanding in craftsmanship. Some of the better companies who made silvered glass of high quality include Hugo Wolf of Iglau and Scheinost of Bohemia.

The firm of A. Scheinost, which was founded in 1866, apparently produced silvered glass products that were of the finest quality. This luxury glass was popular in its day, and readily collected by patrons with an appreciation for the finer things. As such, products from these makers were exhibited at the Vienna Exposition held in 1873.

A great amount of silvered glass made in Bohemia was exported to England and the United States and sold through importers such as the wholesale firm of Silber & Fleming in Victorian England.

In short, the fabrication of double-walled and decorated silvered glass enjoyed the longest production run in Bohemia and Germany, since documentation supports manufacture there from around 1845 until at least 1920. The vases, beakers, compotes, and other items pictured in the following chapters will serve to illustrate the incredible variety of design methods, as well as the artistic merit of silvered glass made in Bohemia.

The actual formation of some Bohemian silvered mercury glass objects involved the use of a mold. Although there were free-blown items such as cups, goblets, and other wares, some of the vase forms and surface patterns, including ribs and panels, could have only been made by using some type of a mold press. Blown-molded silvered glass objects were an important part of the scope of items made, which included glass figures. A religious figurine included in this book, and thought to be of St. Ann, bears the molded mark of J.J.& Co., for Josef Janke, Haida, Bohemia, which produced these figures, as well as some tableware and candlesticks.

The varied and specific methods of decoration are certainly worthy of individual exploration, for they contribute much to help determine the country of origin and help with attribution.

Surface Engraving

Depending on the grade of "metal" or glass to be worked, some Bohemian-made silvered glass was engraved in a manner consistent with the general Biedermeier style of the 1820s through the 1840s. The task of engraving involves a technique that actually abrades the surface of the glass. Revolving copper wheels were used for that purpose. Using a formula containing oil and abrasive grit, such as pumice, the workman held the piece to be engraved upwards against the wheel. Multiple wheels, in various sizes, were necessary to execute the fine cutting that provides depth and dimension to the design. Engraving is one of the most difficult methods to decorate glass. A skilled engraver must possess considerable dexterity as well as artistic talent, in order to be successful at his craft. Engraved designs, which were actually unpolished surface cuttings, appear frosty whitish-gray, and were extremely well suited to silvered glass, as the patterns contrasted beautifully against the shiny silver surface. Further exploration of this particular art will be provided in the section about American silvered glass.

Some Bohemian-made beakers were engraved with depictions of buildings, trees, and landscapes from the so-called "spas" or resorts of the nineteenth century. Buildings, monuments, or important landmarks from the famous city of Carlsbad, for example, were often engraved in stylistic fashion, and sold as keepsakes. In addition, other personalized engraved items were often given as commemorative pieces. However, engraving was limited, and most Bohemian silvered glass items were decorated by the use of other techniques.

Etching and Frosting

By definition, etching is a method that actually corrodes the surface of the glass producing an effect that looks similar to engraving, at least in color. There were several types of etching used on silvered glass, including acid application that rendered a specific pattern or design, and vapor acid matting to a large area of the piece. Treatment with acid produced a surface that looks like frosted satin, in a matte finish. In both cases, some form of hydrofluoric acid was used. Another technique involved a wax resist method, where the entire surface was coated with a substance to "resist" the acid treatment, and the design was created by drawing or tooling through the layer of wax or resist material, then applying the acid treatment which would "etch" the exposed areas, and then removing the "resist" material which would reveal the applied design in white against the untreated silver mirror surface.

Although there is some speculation that a type of sand "blasting" could have been employed as an etching method for silvered glass, the thin surfaces of the glass would have probably precluded this technique.

The acid-etched matte ground, which contrasted nicely with the shiny surface of the untreated areas, was often the "canvas" onto which further decorations were applied. Many pieces show painted birds, butterflies, or gold enamel work that is much more aesthetically pleasing against the softened silver surface. Other examples appear to have been etched using a template or stencil. In such cases, the shiny surface is blocked with a thin tin plate with a design cut through. An application of etching solution is applied, and when the stencil plate is removed, the design remains.

Granulate Application

Although the majority of Bohemian silvered glass appears, at first examination, to be etched by conventional methods, another specialized decorating technique that was used far more frequently involved the application of glass powders, which were made of finely ground crystal. During tactile examination, it is possible to feel the raised and markedly gritty surface of the birds, flowers, ferns, leaves, vines, and palms that form much of the designs found on Bohemian German silvered mercury glass. In this method, called "Granulate-Technik" in German, it is likely that a glue-like substance was applied to the surface of the article, either by hand, or, in designs with intricate patterns, by the use of a resist-template. The template, much like a stencil, was probably placed over the surface of the object, and the glue-like material applied so that it covered the areas to be coated with the granulate particles. Likely made of pulverized quartz or other ground materials, the powder was dusted onto the object, similar to confectioners' sugar. Once the template was removed, or, in the case of freehand application, coated evenly with the glass particulates, the piece was fired in low heat to allow the design to "set" by slight melting. This would account for the occasional wear that is found on these designs. Surface etching, which deteriorates the glass itself, could not rub off in the conventional sense. In addition, the raised surfaces of this method were far more prone to surface soiling, and some antique examples often appear brown. Careful cleaning may restore the white color, and this will be discussed in a later chapter, which includes methods to clean mercury glass.

There appears to have been some variation in the actual granulate formula used, because certain pieces appear to have been decorated with crushed crystals, almost like granulated sugar, as evidenced by the inherent sparkle in the pattern. Other pieces must have been decorated with a highly pulverized granulate that resembles fine powder, which makes the pattern look more like conventional etching.

Enamel Work

The application of color, as well as gold and silver enameling, was a frequent method of decoration. Applied directly to the glass surface, usually over an acid vapor-matted area, the piece was then re-fired to fix the enamel. In spite of this re-heating method, which helped to bond the decoration to the surface, some examples show wear to the enameled areas. Often applied as bands that highlight the intricate turns and knops of the stem or used around the rim and foot of shapely vases and goblets, most of the enamel work was executed with great skill. Enameling was an important design method employed in the artistry of silvered glass.

Glass "Jewels"

One of the more fascinating and truly rare decorating techniques used on silvered glass was the application of glass beads, or jewels. Round or flat colored glass embellishments in various shapes and sizes were applied to the glass surface, and were often shaped or cut to resemble precious gemstones. On other pieces, tiny multicolored glass beads were used as accents to add detail and dimension to engraved or etched patterns. In either case, jeweled silvered glass objects are quite dazzling to behold! Uncommon to find, these pieces are very rare and as such, highly valuable.

Painting

Surface painting on mercury glass often varies in quality. Exports to Victorian England and America often featured large and showy flowers, using multiple colors and shading, that were subject to wear when used or cleaned. In terms of technical merit, painted silvered glass items often appear rather amateurish, even if the pigments have survived. Considering the increased leisure time of the Victorian upper classes in the last decades of the nineteenth century, it is possible that silvered glass blanks were not only finished for completion by secondary artists at home, but sold outright to be decorated by hobbyists. It is well known that porcelains and other items were sold to crafters, and that many ladies pursued such undertakings at home in the late nineteenth century. Based on the naïve renderings found on some objects, this speculation seems highly probable.

Staining and Flashing

Many mercury glass vases, compotes, and goblets are described as "gold-washed" and indeed, while no real gold was used, the contrast of the gold to silver resulted in a piece of unrivaled brilliance. During the initial cooling or annealing phase, chemical stains were applied to the semi-molten surface of the glass objects. In other pieces that were completely annealed and finished, a light coat flashing in a contrasting color, such as ruby red, was applied over a metal stencil. When the plate was removed, the intaglio silver pattern remained. A final step was the addition of paint to outline or highlight the design, which often included stylized leaves, trees, and birds.

Sealing Methods

Double-walled silvered glass objects almost always involved the use of a sealing device. In fact, many inventors pursued patent protection regarding a specific sealing methodology, although copying was uncontrollable. Immigration patterns, especially among glass workers, may have contributed to the similarity of some sealing work. Bohemian and German silvered mercury glass, as a rule, never used a cork as a seal. The most common sealing method involved the use of a circular piece of metal or cardboard that was affixed over the pontil scar hole, covered with a round glass disc, and then glued or cemented into place. The simple cardboard closures under seal appear to have been painted grayish silver, presumably to hide the characteristics of their appearance. In most of these seals, the glass is often uneven and the cement is usually visible. There is a roughness around the edges of the pontil scar, and it would seem that no particular attention was paid to this finishing step. Most of the sealing methods used in Bohemia were sufficient to close the piece, but rather inadequate regarding the aesthetic detail. In some examples, the type of glass used in the sealing discs is actually different than the glass of the piece itself. Upon close inspection, the glass discs, although original, are made from glass with a greenish tint, in contrast to the clear, colorless glass of the object itself.

In some other pieces, there seemed to be more care rendered with respect to the final seal.

Items attributed to the firm of Hugo Wolf, for example, have a metal seal stamped "HW" that was fitted over the pontil scar, and covered with a round glass disc. In these objects, the discs were ground to fit the polished pontil opening, which is quite similar to the method described in the English patent by Varnish and Thomson. This is evident in the comparison of seals from piece to piece.

These sealing methods were sufficient, as long as the pieces were not submerged in water, for the loosening of the cement and resultant loss of the seal, opened the piece to atmospheric effects that degraded the silvering. We are all too familiar with the unsightliness of mercury glass items that show a loss of the interior silver coating.

The subject of sealing requires certain consideration, especially in terms of establishing the value of an object. The presence of the original seal is desirable and will often correlate to the general condition of the piece. However, there are some mercury glass items that have retained their original seal, but show deterioration in the forms of spotting, cloudiness, or flaking loss. Other pieces found without a seal have retained much of their original luster.

Perhaps some makers were more proficient in the process to create the silver coating, for this important step, which is often missed by other investigators, involved the heat-treatment of the vessel to 'set' the silver coat before pouring out the excess argentine fluid. This 'baking-on' method insured the adherence of the silvering to the interior glass surface. The silvering solution was not just poured in, swirled to coat the interior, and then emptied out. The chemical characteristics of silver nitrate, however used in an amalgam, require this additional step.

Glass silvered and decorated in Bohemia was made in abundance, and much was exported to England and the United States. Collectors can readily find examples of sphere-shaped candleholders marked Czechoslovakia. The value of silvered mercury glass items depends largely on the quality of design, rarity of form, size of the piece, and general condition. Objects with cracks or glass damage have little value, and tolerance for the loss of silvering is somewhat subjective, depending on individual taste. The presence or absence of a maker's hallmark is important to some collectors, but the vast majority of mercury glass items were not marked. Pairs of vases or candlesticks are generally more valuable, and height is certainly a consideration. Pieces created with unusual decorative elements, such as those embellished with "jewels" or items exhibiting an outstanding general quality usually command premium prices. Like other types of artistic glass, the inherent appeal is truly individual.

Silvered glass made in Bohemia and Germany clearly represents the most varied and innovative methods of decorating when compared to the wares of England and the United States. Many items are unique and therefore, quite valuable.

England

Although there is no known documentation of experimentation in England analogous to the story from Bohemia, London chemist Thomas Drayton registered a process for silvering glass blanks in 1848. British patent number 12,358 provides a silvering formula, including "hartshorn" or ammonia, nitrate of silver, three ounces of water, and three ounces of spirit (the preferred substance was wine) to be mixed, settled, filtered, and applied to surfaces of glass. Although Drayton's formula apparently worked to silver surfaces, the coating quickly deteriorated. However, in December of 1849, another patent for silvering glass vessels was granted jointly to Frederick Hale Thomson and Edward Varnish that was based on the Drayton formula. Specifically addressing both the formation of the double-walled vessels as well as the sealing method, patent number 12,905 proved successful. The accompanying illustrations in the patent referenced an inkstand and "fingerglass" which was simply a footed goblet. The methods patented included one technique for blowing a double-walled vessel in one piece, and another for the creation of two layers of glass that were joined together and sealed. References to the Thomson-Varnish patent method vary widely from publication to publication. Another patent, issued to Frederick

Hale Thomson and Thomas Robert Mellish, included refinements in the use of colored plating and decorative cutting. The specification for the Thomson-Mellish patent, which was number 13,229 granted in 1850, describes methods for "cutting, staining, silvered and fixing articles of glass."

Although the following article, "Gold and Silver Glass" from the August 31, 1850, issue of *Scientific American* does not identify Thomson, Varnish, or Mellish specifically, the reference is unmistakable:

"A new method of manufacturing ornamental glass has lately been discovered, which presents the brilliant appearance of highly polished gold and silver. This mode of 'silvering' glass is a new invention, which is now being carried on by a company in London. The various articles are blown of two different thickness of glass throughout, and the silver is deposited upon the two interior surfaces of the double hollow glass vessel. The silver is deposited from a solution of that metal by the reducing agency of saccharine solutions; in short, the process is entirely a chemical one. The double hollow vessels are hermetically

sealed, and thus the silver deposit is protected from wear and from atmospheric influences. The brilliant silver deposit being seen through the colored glass, communicates to that substance, in a curiously illusive manner, the apperence (sic) of being entirely formed of gold and silver itself. When the glass is cut, the brilliancy of the silver is heightened; and, on the other hand, when the glass is ground, the effect of frosted silver is produced. By staining, and the employment of variously colored glasses, the effect is modified in variety of ways, thus, with certain yellow glasses, the effect of gold is produced; with deep and ruby glass, colored metallic lustres, equal to the effect of the plumage of birds, are obtained. As every form into which glass can be blown is silvered with facility, the extent to which this beautiful invention can be carried is perfectly unlimited. The new process extends to flower vases, chimney ornaments, and in fact, to every article usually made of glass. For ornaments it presents all the lustrous brilliancy of highly polished gold and silver, at a great reduction of cost, and for imitating jewelry and illuminations it will far surpass anything known. In fact, the invention is at present IN ITS INFANCY, and promises soon to fill the house of the middle classes, usually destitute of brilliant ornaments, with cheap articles presenting all the striking appearance of costly plate, etc."

Later in the same year, in another article from *Scientific American* written for the October 26, 1850, issue entitled "The Manufacture of Fine Glass in England," there is much editorial opinion offered about the virtues of silvered glass. In fact, one realizes that the generous use of description, often with multiple adjectives and elaborate language seemed necessary in this era because of the absence of image and color illustration:

"In one department, viz. silvering glass, the English have attainted a superiority over every other nation...This kind of glass is made in Berners Street, London, but a process lately invented and patented by Mr. Hale Thompson: (sic) he discards all the old methods of using essential oils, and coats all his surfaces, flat or curved, the smallest toilet bottle or largest vase with pure silver, far more brilliantly than the amalgum (sic) applied to ordinary looking glasses, and can never become tarnished or impaired except by destroying it. The metallic radiance of this deposit imparts a combined sparkle and warmth, quite beyond the Bohemian, which is comparatively merely pretty and tinselly; and there is the important factor that British glass is far superior to anything elsewhere produced. Hence, taking quality of material, the English is on a par with Bohemian in price, and the beautiful and unique silvering is so much additional gain. The richness and purity of British crystal admit splendor and voluptuousness of dyes that satisfy the most exigent fastididiousness; hence the purple, sapphires, pinks, vermilions, pearls, bronzes, etc., in short, every chromatic hue thrown up by this new argentine reflection, have the gorgeous glow the antique Venetian glass, the secret of which is now a lost art; but whereas the Venetian absorbed the light, and had to be held up to it before its softened beauties were revealed, the English silvered glass flashed back the light, and is seen best at night, or when surrounding objects are in comparative gloom. Another characteristic never attempted since the discover of glass itself by Hermes, the Syrian, is embossing — that is, to the eye, for it is an optical delusion, there being no raised surface to the touch, though the appearance is that of pure solid silver, either dead or frosted, burnished or in high relief, or sunken. It is impossible to exaggerate the results of this, applied to finger-plates for doors, enrichments for cabinets, panels, cornice mouldings, or combinations with ivory, gilding, or rare woods, to all which, and innumerable other purposes, this invention is adapted. At these glass silvering works vases are made which are as high as $3,000.00 per pair, nine-tenths of the cost is incurred in designing and engraving alone. In design, English glass has made immense progress and the goblets, epergnes, candelabra, wine coolers, etc., now referred to, are equal of vertu in classic beauty of form and of commercial importance, or suitability to the taste of the age. But as if to exemplify the adage, that the closer to simplicity the greater the art, perhaps the chef d' oeuvres in this manufacture are mirror globes, of plain silvered surface, all sizes, from two to thirty inches in diameter, from half a pint to forty gallons. These, placed on bronze figures, as an atlas or eagle, attached to chandeliers, or on a sideboard or mantelpiece, are a most striking appendage to the drawing room or banquet hall.

We have, as Americans, done but little in the manufacture of fine ornamental glass, but the time is approaching when we will not be behind any nation in this branch of art. At present, we import a great deal, but this will not be the case long; we have a strong evidence form making this assertion, in viewing the fine display of crystal ornamental glass vessels, displayed at the Fair of the Institute, by the BROOKLYN GLASS COMPANY. Some of the articles displayed are splendid — the colors and designs are highly credible to the company and the artisans engaged in the manufacture. We consider glass as a great civilizer, both as it respects its application to the arts, and its use for ornamental purposes. We do not know but like good rods, the amount of glass used in any country, may be taken as a proper evidence of its civilization."

To properly understand the method by which hollow double-walled blown glass was made, it is necessary to provide information about the technique of glassblowing itself. The task of glassblowing is reasonably explained as follows:

When a batch of melted glass, comprised of ingredients as previously discussed, reaches the appropriate temperature, a worker, using a blowpipe, which is a hollow metal tube about four feet long, collects, or "gathers" a small ball of molten glass on the end of the blowpipe. This worker, also known as a "gatherer" blows a little air into the pipe, which begins to slightly inflate the hot ball of glass at the end. The gatherer continues to blow and rotate the blowpipe, and when the temperature of the glass cools by hundreds of degrees, he rolls the hot glass on a special table with a metal surface, called a "marvering" table, which consolidates, and helps shape the piece. The gatherer then hands the blowpipe to the blower, who continues to twirl the pipe while blowing more air into the piece, thus working it into the desired shape, such as a vessel. If the glass becomes too cool, the blowpipe is passed to another worker, known as the "servitor" who reheats the glass in the glory hole of the furnace. The blower continues to work the vessel, and if the rim is to be finished by the blower, the servitor attaches a long, flat-topped iron rod called a pontil to the end of the piece, with a small piece of molten glass, and the blowpipe is now cracked off. The workman completes the vessel, and then, the pontil rod is cracked off, leaving the familiar pontil scar.

According to Charles R. Hajdamach's summary in British Glass (British Glass, 1800 – 1914, England, 1991), which was written after review of a video showing an experiment conducted at the International Glass Center at Brierley Hill, and based on the Varnish goblet in the Broadfield House Museum, the variation necessary to produce a hollowed vessel involves two blowpipes and a concerted effort on the part of a team of workmen. Basically, the first workman begins with one gather of glass, allowing it to cool slightly, and then obtains a second gather of glass to form the bowl first, then the stem. It is necessary to maneuver the glass with great care in order to achieve uniformity in the hollow shape, which was no easy task considering the formation of balusters or knops on the stem. A further blowing then forms the foot, which is shaped further, with additional controlled blowing to create a small ball at the end of the foot, which is then cracked off creating a hole at the base. Another blowing iron with more hot glass is attached exactly over the formed hole. The glass was then cracked off the first blowpipe, and the top, which was roughly opened, was manipulated using pucellas, sealed, then reheated to smooth the closure. The glass continued to be shaped and then, once held upright, the molten top slumped down, creating the double wall. It should be noted that all silvered glass goblets illustrated in this book, including the examples made in the United States, have a discernable bumpy area on the inside bottom of the bowl, which supports the aforementioned process.

Another defining feature of English silvered glass was that it was made from lead glass. The history of true lead glass can be traced back to the year 1673 when Englishman George Ravenscroft developed a formula using lead that produced glass that was much more clear, brilliant, and heavy, which allowed for cutting and engraving. Lead silicilates including red lead or litharge, improved the quality of glass. Glass containing lead is also more resonant, and when struck lightly, rings like a bell. Lead itself is very heavy, and so the vessels blown double walled are actually of noticeable weight when held. This fact dispels another commonly held belief that silvered mercury glass is "light-weight."

As mentioned earlier, glass that was blown double walled and silvered, regardless of origin, and initially described or marketed as "silvered" is referred to as "mercury glass."

In addition to the descriptions in *Scientific American*, there are references to displays of silvered glass at the Great Crystal Palace Exposition, held in 1851, which took place in London, England. The premise of the Exposition was the joining together of art, science, and industry to explore the myriad contributions of exhibitors from many lands. Attended by British royalty and thousands of visitors, the Crystal Palace housed an extraordinary array of items that represented a scope of manufactured articles never seen before. The exhibits included the finest glass offerings available at the time, including objects made in England, Bohemia, France, Belgium, and the United States.

There are many written recordings of this unprecedented event, but the most highly illustrated and undoubtedly one of the best versions may be *The Illustrated Catalogue* by The Art Journal, published in 1852.

With essays including the science of the exhibition and lessons on taste by leading authorities at the time, the following brief narrative passage accompanying the line-drawn illustrations of the silvered glass vessels on display there, stated the following:

"The Centre-dish and two Vases which occupy this column are from the establishment of Mr. Mellish, of London. They are of glass, silvered by Mr. Hale Thomson's process, described at length in the Art-Journal for March of the present year, (1851) to which we would refer such of our readers as feel an interest in this truly beautiful manufacturing Art. There is a peculiarity in the manufacture of the glass used by Mr. Mellish in his process, which merits particular notice, from its novelty and ingenuity; all the articles, whether goblets, vases, or others, have double sides, between which the silver solution is precipitated."

From the same publication, in an essay on the science of the exhibition from Robert Hunt, Esq., comes the following:

"The subject of silvering glass is a curious one — and the examples of the most recent improvements of precipitating silver with grape sugar, found in the contributions to the Exhibition, are excellent….In immediate connection with the process, because illustrated by it, we may refer to the brilliancy of colour produced in our English flint glass. Since the glass-maker has succeeded in rivaling the Bohemian in his tints, the reflection through these from the silvered surface, teaches us that colours are produced which are curious in their effects, and physically interesting…We often find a glass, yellow by transmitted light, which exhibits a blue colour at certain angles of reflection, and the same is often, although less frequently, seen with the ruby glasses. By the silvering process, this reflected colour is considerably exalted, and this dichroism is very pleasingly illustrated."

In "Tallis's History and Description of the Crystal Palace and the Exhibition of the World's Industry in 1851, which was printed and published by John Tallis and Company, London and New York, there is an entire section devoted to the discovery of glass, and other topics related to glass, including the following:

"Specimens of the beautiful silvered glass lately become so fashionable, and which has formed so ornamental a feature at various public banquets, were exhibited by Messrs. Varnish, of Berners-street. The silvered globes were already familiar to the public, but there were various other articles, such as a chess-table, goblets, curtain-poles, etc., which showed the great adaptability of the material to ornamental purposes."

The article goes on to describe the brilliancy of metallic colors of the "metal," particularly in Bohemian glass, and states:

"In the articles exhibited by Mr. Varnish and Mr. Mellish, these colours were well shown. Messrs. Powell and Co., Whitefriars, manufactured most of the glass exhibited by them and this itself is presented a noticeable peculiarity. All the glass was double, the object, of this being to enable the patentees to fill the inside with a solution of nitrate of silver, to which grape sugar was added, when all the silver held in solution was deposited in a beautiful film of revived silver over every part of the glass. This silvering on the interior wall of the glass (globes, vases, and numerous other articles were shown to be susceptible to the process) has the property of reflecting back through the glass all the light, which falls on the surface — whereas ordinarily some is transmitted, and only a small portion reflected. This exalts many of the colours in a striking manner, and not only does it exalt the colours, but the dichromism of the glass is curiously displayed. Much of the red and yellow glass thus assumes an opalescent tinge of blue, which, in some examples, is not unpleasing. We greatly admired some of the coloured examples of this process, but we cannot think that pure white glass — the beauty of which is its transparency is in any respect improved by silvering."

Reviewers, however verbose in their exploration of the subject of silvered glass, appeared to offer different opinions on the subject. What is notable, however, is the reference to silvered glass globes that "were already familiar to the public." While the Varnish and Thomson patent appeared to describe tableware, not much is known about globes having been produced there. English silvered glass, as described by the patent granted to Edward Varnish and Hale Thomson, was produced for a limited time, from about 1849 to 1853. For this reason, surviving pieces are extremely rare.

Fabrication of the double-walled vessels that were further embellished by the use of colorful overlay, and cut to silver, was certainly labor intensive. Some English examples were wheel engraved, and these fine products must have influenced the glassmakers of New England, who seemed to expound on the variety of designs and patterns created by engraving.

In other English examples, the use of colored glass itself, such as in the green master salt illustrated on page 132, present another desirable form for consideration. In addition to the familiar casing, colored glass items of every hue were treated to the silvering process. Fantastic and colorful, the pieces are quite brilliant, and come in blue, green, red, pink, and even purple, or amethyst. Tableware and vases were made in abundance, and must have been highly regarded by the Victorian classes who sought decorative objects of artistic beauty to display in their homes.

Whether plain or cased, there is no question as to the superior grade of the English wares when compared to the silvered glass pieces produced in Bohemia and on the continent. Additionally, silvered glass made in England was produced for only about five years. For those reasons, English silvered glass is usually difficult to find, and when offered for sale, is priced accordingly.

Sealing Methods

The English have always had a great propensity toward marking their wares, and the silvered glass pieces patented by Varnish and Thomson are easily identifiable because of their hallmark. There are several variations of the mark, although they contain the names of Varnish or Thomson in some combination with the words "patent" and "London." Since Varnish and Thomson obtained the first patent, held jointly, it is hard to speculate as to the exact reason for these differences. From the illustrated collection in this book there are several examples, with the variations as follows:

A master salt marked: E. VARNISH & CO. PATENT LONDON
A plain, silvered chalice marked: THOMSON'S PATENT LONDON
A plain, silvered vase marked: HALE THOMSON'S PATENT LONDON

In all cases, the lettering was stamped on what appears to be a metal disc that was fitted over the pontil opening underfoot and covered with a round glass disc.

Of note, is that the inclusion of "& CO." appears only with the name of E. Varnish. Thomson's name, on the other hand, at least on the items included in this survey, does not bear that distinction. An additional mark that is found includes W. Lund, but no examples are included in this collection.

There are written references to Thomas Mellish, who was also quite possibly a retailer, in the aforementioned exhibition of 1851, which included displays of Varnish glass. There are some who believe Varnish and Thomson were also involved primarily in the retail business, but there has been no conclusive evidence to prove this assumption.

It is true that the blanks used for the silvering process were made at James Powell and Sons, Whitefriars, London, but the inclusion of Varnish and Thompson in the hallmark appears to indicate their direct involvement in the more important aspect of manufacture, however unclear.

The English sealing method was done with great skill and precision, as the glass discs fit snugly into place, with little, if any, evidence of cement. This technique required exact measuring to insure the proper match between the diameters of the aperture as well as the glass disc seal. Both the pontil scar and edges of the foot-hole must have been ground or polished, for the finished sealed surface is completely smooth to the touch. The result afforded extraordinary protection against the elements, as revealed in the brilliancy of surviving pieces. It is unusual to find any English silvered glass that has lost its luster, as compared to the glass made in Bohemia or the United States.

Silvered glass made in England is probably the most valuable, when compared to Bohemia, other Continental makers, and even the United States. This is attributable to its distinct rarity, because of both the short production time and the exquisite quality of each piece. As such, pieces found command prices that are usually in the hundreds, if not thousands of dollars.

The United States

Double-walled silvered glass was made in the United States from the early 1850s to the late 1870s.

The history of silvered glass made in the United States is a natural part of the general story involving the evolution of American glassmaking. Up to now, the study and reference to silvered mercury glass and its inclusion within the context of glass manufacturing in America has been both capricious and arbitrary. Some authors treat the ware merely as a footnote to the late nineteenth century era of so-called "art glass," while others have ignored the topic completely. In spite of such treatment, the story of silvered glass has historic importance within the scope of study for serious students of Americana. The inherent characteristics, including its beauty and quality craftsmanship, deserve proper attention. Although utilitarian in form, most pieces were probably made for display. Some authors refer to silvered glass as the first type of true "art glass."

Blown and tooled using the old and traditional methods inherent in handmaking, American silvered glass preserved the blowers and engravers art, and filled the course along the timeline from the middle years of the nineteenth century. Around that time period, from about 1825 to 1850, another method of glass production caused a deviation away from the important enterprise of glassblowing. After the momentous invention of the glass-pressing machine, some companies did not survive. Thankfully, the demand for silvered glassware may have helped workmen to maintain their skills, and to continue gainful employment in their respective professions.

There has been much confusion about American silvered glass. Fortunately, there have been several authors who have provided scholarly contributions by means of authoritative research, which has helped, in fact, to support this very endeavor. These writers have correctly included the topic within the proper context of mid-nineteenth century blown glass.

The glassmakers in America were rich in diversity, and many companies, both major and minor, contributed to the success of the new industry. At the beginning of the nineteenth century, there were only a few notable glass firms. After the first few decades of the nineteenth century, glass companies grew almost exponentially, and the numerous glass factories that opened in lower New England enjoyed much competition.

Again, silvered glass produced in America was made free blown, and wares were created in shapes that did not deviate appreciably from the styles and forms of the pitchers, compotes, and bowls that were blown of flint glass and made in the second through fourth decades of the nineteenth century. In fact, all American silvered glass was made from flint glass, which gives the finished pieces considerable weight when compared to the more lightweight Bohemian products that were made from leadless glass. Flint glass formulas vary from maker to maker, and the ingredients and proportions per recipe were well guarded from company to company. One formula called for red lead or litharge, sand, pearl ash, nitre, manganese, and arsenic. There were many other variations, but all contained lead.

There are undeniable similarities between blown, double-walled silvered glass and the plain, single-layer blown glass shapes of the earlier decades. Silvered glass pitchers usually have a clear applied glass handle that was finished by crimping on the bottom where it attached to the body. This feature is identical to many examples made from 1820 to 1840, by Thomas Cains's South Boston Flint Glass Works. The blown shape of these "Cains" style pitchers, with their bulbous body, round ample foot, and tooled spout are similar in shape to the silvered glass pitchers made a few short decades later. There is also a marked comparison to pitchers made in South Jersey, as well as in Pennsylvania.

Many American silvered glass pieces were expertly engraved. As mentioned previously in this chapter, glass formulas were inherently important in the determination of form, function, and design. The heavier, more resonant flint glass was perfectly suited for wheel engraving, and many silvered glass items were beau-

tifully embellished with the neoclassic motifs so familiar in the post Federal style. In fact, the use of the wreath and simple initials, which are found in many silvered glass goblets, is very similar to the engraved designs attributed to John Amelung. Bohemian influences were evident in most aspects of engraving, and the appearance of grapevines, tendrils, and stylized flowers impacted the design elements. Thus, the wheel-engraved motifs, which were executed by such notable artists as Louis Vaupel, Henry Leighton, and Henry S. Fillebrown for the New England glass company, follow the proliferation of decorative designs resulting from the influence of both the Anglo-Irish and Bohemian style.

Both plain and wheel engraved American silvered glass tableware is a distinct and beautiful product. Blown with simple, classic lines, and decorated with elegant, tasteful designs, the pieces were certainly much more

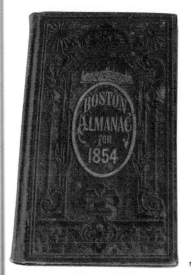

Glass Manufactories.

H. P. COCHRANE,

Manufacturer of Cut and Fancy Glass and Britannia Ink Stands, Adhesive Mucilage, Homœopathic, Druggists' Glass and Britannia Ware, Coffin Trimmings, &c.

Corner of Lancaster and Causeway Streets, Boston.

Bay State Glass Co. 54 Kilby
Boston Glass Co 97 Water
Boston & Sandwich Glass Co., 51 Federal [caster, (inkstands)
Cochrane H. P. Causeway, c. Lancaster
Jarves G. D. & Cormerais, 51 Federal
N. E. Glass Co., 45 Batterymarch
Page & Robbins, 189 & 191 State & 86 & 88 Central
Phœnix Glass Co. 78 Water
Rogers G. W. & Co. 38 Canal
Russell Jas. D. & Co., Second, n. A
SUMNERS & CO. 137 Washington, see advertisement on page 119.
Union Glass Co., 36 Kilby
Young A. E. 54 Kilby

Grain Measurer.
Bradford R. B. 15 E. Clinton
Davis N. 121 Commercial

Grinding Mills.
Am. Grist Mill Co. 2 Haymarket sq.

Grindstones.
Lombard & Co. 13 Lewis wharf
Seaman J. T. & Co. 293 Comm'l
Sprague, Soule & Co. 10 T wharf

Gunny Cloth and Bags
Chipman W. 81 Commercial
Loud W. F. 49 India wharf
Kimball D. & Son, 106 Fulton

Boston Almanac – Business Directory. Author's collection.

austere than the bright and elaborate English ware. The quality of the glass itself, with its resonance and brilliancy, made American silvered glass more elegant when compared to the items made in Bohemia and Europe.

Made in utilitarian shapes, silvered glass tableware in every form was produced by many greater Boston area companies including the New England Glass Company of Cambridge, Massachusetts; the famous Boston and Sandwich Glass Company of Sandwich, Cape Cod, Massachusetts; the Union Glass Company of Somerville, Massachusetts; the Bay State Glass Company of East Cambridge, Massachusetts; the American Glass Company of South Boston, Massachusetts; and perhaps most important of all, the Boston Silver Glass Company established in Cambridge, Massachusetts, by John Haines. The fact that a glass company was created almost exclusively for the manufacture of silvered glass gives credence to the popularity of the ware.

The Union Glass Company published a wholesale price list of silvered glass products in April 1874, describing various pieces as follows:

SALTS:	SUGARS AND COVERS:	CREAM PITCHERS
High foot, plain, per dozen – $4.50	Plain, per dozen – $15.00	Plain, per dozen – $15.00
High foot, engraved, per dozen – $6.00	Engraved, per dozen – $18.00	Engraved, per dozen – $18.00

In addition to covered sugars, pitchers, and footed master salts, there were bowls in all sizes, butters and covers, candlesticks, celeries, cheese plates and covers, cigar holders, mugs, paperweights, spoon holders, strawberry dishes, and even ash holders.

An invoice from the American Glass Company of South Boston, dated February 1854, lists silvered salts, covered sugars, and spoon holders sold by the half-dozen.

All of these companies, which operated in Massachusetts, shared commonalities that contributed to the development of silvered glass in the period lasting from about 1851 to 1880. Their production of silvered glass is authenticated through billheads, trade cards, or catalog listings, and in some cases, by documented provenance. Glassmakers comprised a small, tight-knit community, and skilled craftsman moved from company to company, often competing against former employers.

Outside of New England, there were several companies who made silvered glass, including The Franklin Flint Glass Works of Philadelphia, Pennsylvania; Dithridge and Company's Fort Pitt Glass Works of Pittsburgh, Pennsylvania; the Keystone Flint Glass Company, of Pittsburgh, Pennsylvania; as well as the firm of Gillender & Sons, Philadelphia, Pennsylvania.

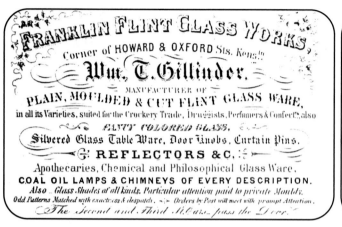

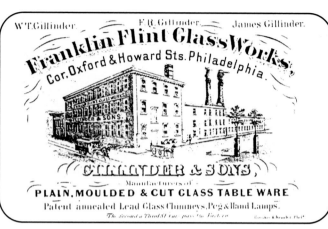

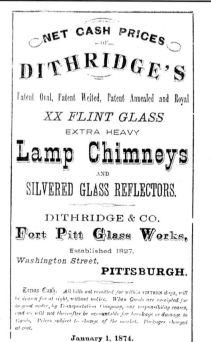

Courtesy of the Museum of American Glass, Millville, NJ.

SILVERED GLASS GLOBES AND STANDS.

	PER DOZ.
4 inch, Globes and Stands..........	$ 6 50
5 " " "	7 50
6 " " "	9 00
7 " " "	12 00
8 " " "	15 00
9 " " "	20 00
10 " " "	30 00
12 " " "	40 00
13 " " "	56 00
14 " " "	75 00
15 " " "	100 00
16 " " "	130 00
17 " " "	160 00
18 " " "	190 00
20 " " "	250 00

Dithridge's Patent Globe Bouquet Holders.

	PER DOZ.
4½ inch Bouquet.....	$18 00
6 " "	24 00
7 " "	30 00
8 " "	35 00
9 " "	45 00
10 " "	60 00
12 " "	80 00
13 " "	100 00
14 " "	120 00
15 " "	150 00

Silvered Glass Curtain Pins.

	PER DOZ.
1 inch, Plain, Rosette, or Pearl,......	$ 1 25
1½ " " " "	1 50
2 " " " "	2 00
2½ " " " "	2 25
3 " " " "	2 75
3½ " " " "	3 00
4 " " " "	3 50

FLORENCE FLASKS, for Dentists' Use.

1 quart,...... ....
3 pints,........ ....

Silver Glass Mortars and Pestles.

4 inch, each, ...	$2 00
6 " "	3 50
8 " "	6 00
9 " "	7 50
10 " "	8 50

Courtesy of the Museum of American Glass, Millville, NJ.

Silvered glass items in similar shapes are listed in a catalog from the Dithridge & Co. Fort Pitt Glass Works in Pittsburgh, Pennsylvania, dated 1874. In addition to typical tableware forms, other items include card receivers, bouquet vases, match holders, and goblets, all in varying sizes, and priced by the dozen.

The only American company, at least known up to this time, that marked their silvered glass was the New England Glass Company. The New England Glass Company apparently used a round metal plate stamped with "NEG Co." in a sealing method that was quite similar to the Thomson and Varnish process patented in England. Since the New England Glass Company apparently perfected a specific sealing method as described above, it is reasonable to conclude that they probably used that same method exclusively on all their silvered glass ware. One notable exception may be the silvered glass globes on stands, which utilize a simple cork seal. Perhaps the evolution of improved methods at sealing resulted in the use of the metal disc and glass seal, and it is quite conceivable that the New England Glass Company may have used the cork in the initial production of silvered glass.

The New England Glass Company.

John Haines, who was a partner in the Boston Silver Glass Company, was granted patent number 47,101 for silvering glass pitchers, and the date of April 4, 1865, was stamped along the bottom of the metal spout attached to the silvered glass pitcher. Some examples have survived, as the ones illustrated in this book. Other silvered mercury glass items are sealed simply with a cork in the pontil scar, which is usually discovered to have a sharp, unpolished surface. It is presumable that other companies, having employed the additional protection of a paper or foil cover, left the pontil area in its original rough state. Some silvered glass seals show a round, reddish material that appears to be treated paper. Since there is no evidence, as yet, to explain the nuances of sealing used at companies other than New England Glass, it is possible that Sandwich used the red paper-type seal. However, since the Boston Silver Glass Company must have produced a fair amount, the seal could well be attributed to that firm. Without further proof, it is impossible to make a positive attribution, at least by the way of the simple cork and paper seal.

The History of Silvered Mercury Glass — United States

UNITED STATES PATENT OFFICE.

JOHN W. HAINES, OF SOMERVILLE, MASSACHUSETTS.

IMPROVEMENT IN SILVERING GLASS PITCHERS.

Specification forming part of Letters Patent No. **47,101**, dated April 4, 1865.

To all whom it may concern:

Be it known that I, JOHN W. HAINES, of Somerville, in the county of Middlesex, in the State of Massachusetts, have invented a new mode of manufacturing a double glass pitcher with metallic cap for silvering; and I do hereby declare that the following is a full and exact description thereof, reference being had to the accompanying drawing, and to the letters of reference marked therein.

The nature of my invention consists in, after having blown the outside of the glass pitcher (marked A) I drop a solid hot glass on the outside rim, (marked B,) thence expanding it into oval shape by means of suction, produced with the mouth, thus forming two copartments, the inside (marked E) for silvering, the inner side (marked F) for holding domestic liquids.

What I claim as my invention, and desire to secure by Letters Patent, is—

The dropping on of the hot glass on the outside rim of the pitcher, and by means of suction with the mouth, expanding the solid piece of hot glass into oval shape, producing two copartments, as above described.

JOHN W. HAINES.

In presence of—
LUTHER BRIGGS,
HERBERT T. WHITMAN.

J. W. HAINES.
SILVERING GLASS PITCHERS.

No. 47,101.   Patented Apr. 4, 1865.

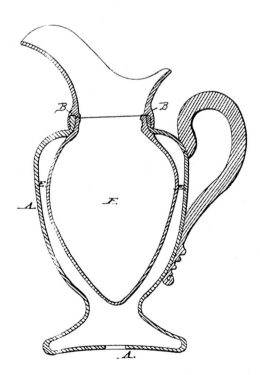

WITNESSES:
Luther Briggs
Herbert T. Whitman

INVENTOR:
John W. Haines

In addition to the companies that produced silvered glass, there were others that apparently sold the ware. A catalog from the Franklin Hallett Lovell Company, printed in 1875, shows all manner of engraved table wares including smoking sets, which included various pieces engraved with the function of the item; a large footed goblet-shaped piece engraved "Segars" for cigars is illustrated along with a holder engraved with the word "Matches" and even a small receptacle with the word "Ashes." It is quite possible that wholesale or retail companies commissioned specialty items from the Pennsylvania makers, as the Lovell Company did not appear to actually produce the glass.

Engraving on American Silvered Glass

Silvered glass, with its shiny mirror surface, was a perfect background to showcase the artistry of fine wheel engraving.

The New England Glass Company provided many of the most skilled glass engravers of the nineteenth century. Louis Vaupel, a German émigré, began work there in 1851. Vaupel was a highly talented and diligent worker. His father was a glasscutter and engraver, who obviously tutored his son in the old traditions. Bringing the Bohemian style, wrought in the tradition of his mountain village, Vaupel executed intricate patterns with a depth and artistry that was unrivaled. Vaupel's sketchbook contained many patterns including stars, "vintage" motifs comprised of grapes, grape leaves, and grapevines, leaf chains, flowers, wreaths, swags, and monograms, just to name a few.

Although the first U.S. patent was granted in 1855, the New England Glass Company showed a variety of silvered glass articles including engraved goblets and one large bowl on foot, presumably a compote, during the 1853 New York Crystal Palace Exhibition. It is reasonable to guess that Louis Vaupel engraved these pieces himself, or directed the other engravers in their pursuits. His work was of the highest quality, and his use of the engravers wheel to shade and accent designs is remarkable. Vaupel apparently engraved silvered glass goblets, for a large, tulip shaped silvered glass presentation piece, including an intricate engraved pattern with the initials "LV" is included in the collection of the Museum of Fine Arts, Boston, Massachusetts.

In 1853, in addition to his direct duties as engraver, he apparently took on the responsibility of managing a new apprentice, which was none other than Henry B. Leighton, who became very proficient at that craft. Leighton, from the family that influenced the Cambridge glass industry, became notable in his own right. Vaupel also managed another apprentice engraver, Henry S. Fillebrown, who has been credited with quality work. Excerpts from the sketchbook of Henry Fillebrown reveal numerous patterns including many with grapevine motifs and garlands, which are very similar if not identical to many specimens of engraved American silvered glass illustrated in the chapters to follow. (See "Henry" goblet page 70.)

Silvered glass was made by the New England Glass Company for years. Reflectors and doorknobs were also an American-made product, but are not explored in this work. However, the other important and unique, contribution to the lexicon of silvered glass products was gazing globes, which will be discussed in Candlesticks and Gazing Globes.

The Boston and Sandwich Glass Company competed with New England in the production of silvered glass. So called "silvered-Sandwich" was made in considerable amounts. Often engraved with the typical "vintage" pattern, the goblets had meandering vines, grape leaves, and tendrils, which varied from piece to piece. Most of these goblets, measuring between 5¾" and 6½" in height, are thick rimmed and rather awkward to actually drink from. Other common motifs include bows, swags, ribbons, and cartouches in the English style, and often contain initials, monograms, and/or dates (illustrated on page 119). A three-piece presentation set engraved December 14, 1864, was probably created as a commemorative set, marking a special occasion. Since these articles, as well as many other goblets engraved with fanciful patterns are not sealed by the New England Glass method, it can be presumed that they may be a Sandwich product. Moreover, silvered glass examples from the Sandwich Glass Museum, with the appropriate provenance, help document engraved work on certain examples. In some examples, there is a distinctive reddish paint, covering the small cork seal. Usually, the pontil area is sharp and rough to the touch.

One lesser-known engraver, who worked at the Sandwich Glass works for a time, was Carl Mattoni, who emigrated from Carlsbad, Bohemia, in 1851. Mentioned in the journal of John Jarves, son of Deming Jarves who founded the famous company, Mattoni apparently engraved a commemorative silvered glass piece that was eventually bequeathed to the Sandwich Historical Society from descendants of the Kern glassmaking family. Although rare to have such a provenance, the existence of the engraved silvered glass piece proves speculation that Sandwich produced silvered glass with a fine quality of engraving. After leaving Sandwich sometime in 1854, he became an independent glass engraver who is listed as "Mattoni, Chas. 38 Milk St." in the Boston Almanac Business Directory for 1859.

Business Directory – Boston Almanac 1859.

Mattoni moved around quite frequently as evidenced by various Boston area addresses listed in directories dating from 1855 to 1870, and it is reasonable to speculate that he may have engraved silvered glass for other companies in the area. Whether at Sandwich or as an independent engraver, patterns and designs attributed to Mattoni are found in many silvered glass articles. The use of garlands, festoons, grape leaves, vines, and flowers is seen in many of Mattoni's pieces.

Pitchers, fitted with a metal spout according to John Haines patent of 1864, often include engraved "vintage," or grapevine designs and give proof that silvered glass produced at the Boston Silver Glass Company was sometimes engraved. When comparing the leaves and tendrils to other vintage patterns, however, the differences are noticeable. Whereas leaves and vines from the New England pieces show clean definition including the presence of veins, the designs from the pitchers and matching pieces are not that well executed, often appearing clumsy or wavy. Of course, the bulbous, and therefore, bulging prominences of glass pitchers may not have been as well suited for engraved decorations as goblets, but the differences are worth mentioning.

Some interesting engraved pieces contain words to describe their actual function, as mentioned earlier in this chapter. One 6" goblet-shaped piece on page 122 is engraved with the word "Segars" which means "Cigars" in Spanish, and so it is a cigar holder. One footed master salt on page 135 says "Mother," and a large presentation bowl on foot on page 123 bears the initials "M.G.T." to "T.G." which was custom made as special gift from a suitor to his lady love.

The presence of engraving on silvered glass goblets seems to confirm that the engraving was performed as a final step, and not, as some have suggested, before the glass was completely silvered. One goblet on page 94 has an engraved oval cartouche, left blank inside, suggesting it was probably made for further inscription. Therefore, it is probable that goblets and other silvered glass vessels were sometimes engraved with a generic design in advance, and then, completed with additional custom engraving upon demand.

Plating or Casing

Plated or cased silvered glass was made in the United States, although production was probably limited, judging from the rarity of items found. In one report describing the products exhibited by the New England Glass Company at the New York Crystal Palace Exhibition in 1853, there is reference to several silvered glass items that were plated, cut, and silvered. The New England glass company had great success with their formula for ruby glass, which was apparently utilized for plating or casing silvered glass, as examples have been found marked "NEG.Co."

The Boston and Sandwich Glass company also produced ruby cased silvered glass, and one example, with wheel engraving along the silvered panels, has been attributed to Carl Mattoni when he worked at that company.

The plated ruby glass cut to silver master salt, illustrated on page 131, has a simple cork in a tiny, unpolished pontil. This would seem a deviation from the more fastidious methods used at the New England Glass Company, and therefore, attribution to Sandwich is more likely.

Sealing

As mentioned, there are several sealing methods used in American silvered glass. The first, which appears to have been perfected by the New England Glass Company, involves an impressed metal seal and glass disc. In this case, the areas were polished, so that no rough edges remained.

In other examples, a simple cork was used and, in many cases, covered with a circular piece of material, possibly treated adhesive cloth, which is sometimes painted red. In both cases, there is no guarantee that the seal is entirely impervious to destruction, for some articles are found with significant silvering loss. Amazingly, many of the simple cork seals have survived and the condition of the silvering is probably as good as the day it was made.

Silvered glass made in the United States is distinct in style, often bearing exquisite wheel engraved designs commensurate with the refined and classic patterns used in other fine blown glass examples made in the mid-nineteenth century. American mercury glass is heavy for its size, and usually classic in form and shape. Engraved and dated commemorative pieces are rare to find, and matching sets are very desirable. Whether plain or engraved, silvered glass made in the United States can be regarded as an important part of the history of glassmaking, and many examples represent the quality of craftsmanship, artistic merit, and design ingenuity so unique in the decorative arts of America.

The most common form of silvered mercury glass is the vase. If you are a collector and own a piece of mercury glass, chances are you have a vase.

Vases proved to be one of the best mediums for decorating, as the large surfaces of the body provided an ample palette for the decorator's art. As discussed earlier, the vase forms were treated to a wide variety of decorating methods, including painting, granulate powder etching, enamel work, applied glass beads to imitate jewels, and acid treatments to provide a satin matte surface.

The vase form evolved from bottle, vessel, and amphora shapes with roots in China, Ancient Egypt, and the Middle East. In the later fifteenth and six-teenth centuries, the traditions of Venice and the influ-ence of the Germanic-Bohemian designs helped to shape the evolution of style. Many glass vase forms were based on ceramic shapes, where utilitarian necessity caused development of vessels to hold water. Vases are taller than wider, and usually have a round-ed shape.

By the nineteenth century, vases were made in a variety of forms and styles. Mercury glass vases can be

round and bulbous shaped or cylindrical and geometric in form. The baluster shape looks like a pear or teardrop, with the widest portion on the lower end, while the reverse-baluster shape has the widest part on top. Most mercury glass vases are based on these two principal styles. In free-blown baluster shapes, the foot and stem was formed during the marvering stage. The glassmaker's tool, or pucellas, was used to aid in shaping. Stri-ation marks in the glass surface support this theory. The neck generally narrows then flares at the rim in both the true baluster and reverse baluster shapes, and some vases have bobbin or ball knops and contoured collars.

While rounded and gracefully graduated balustroid shapes are the most common mercury glass vase form, there are other examples that could have only been made with the use of a mold. Evidently, some derivation of blow molding was used to create the ribbed effect in some pieces. While the glass appears to have defini-tive contours on the outside, the ribbing is hardly discernible on the exterior surface of the double-walled piece. It is reasonable to conclude that the step-by-step fabrication of the vessel, including use of two blowing irons to create the double wall, must have included the use of a mold at some stage before the final finishing. It was possible that the original gather of glass, used to form the base body, was molded while semi-molten, cooled a bit, then removed, re-heated, and continually worked and shaped, thereby comprising the layer that was "slumped" inside the vessel. This explanation would account for the lack of ridge and mold marks on the outside of the piece, but support the visual appearance of ribs on the exterior surface.

The size of the vases illustrated in this chapter range from a diminutive four inches to a colossal nineteen inches tall, but the majority of vases generally average between eight to ten inches in height.

Often made in pairs, vases were probably placed on mantle pieces or arranged on furniture surfaces simply for show. Many of the vases have short interiors that were simply too shallow to hold enough water for flowers. The large, monumental vases known as the "Chinese Chinoserie" (page 47) and the "Jungle Vase" (page 47) have relatively short interior chambers, which are simply too shallow for flowers and water. Moreover, most mercury glass vases were made of non-lead glass, are lightweight, and were therefore impractical to hold anything of weight.

Most silvered glass vases were made in Bohemia, although cased cut to silvered pieces bearing an English hallmark can be found. Large tulip-shaped vessels made in the United States are presumed by form to have been made as vases, but are rare to find. Vases also reveal considerable differences in quality, where workmanship and design vary widely. However, the appeal of silvered mercury glass, regardless of form and its inherent value, can be very subjective. Some Bohemian vases are quite remarkable, showcasing incredible, often exotic decorating techniques that are truly unique. Thus, the value of each vase depends on the rarity, condition, size, and decorative appeal, which vary considerably from piece to piece.

Made in Bohemia third quarter nineteenth century and measuring 10" tall, this free-blown, non-lead glass vase has a well-executed painted bouquet of stylized flowers in red, blue, and shaded green. There are applied gold enamel tendrils and a dragonfly, which contrast vividly against the vapor-acid satin matte ground. Shaped in a rounded cylindrical form with a base collar, the top opening measures 3¾" and the round foot about the same size. The piece retains its original seal, which appears to be silver-colored paper under a round glass disc affixed in the pontil scar underfoot. The piece is in near-original condition showing no evidence of wear or silvering loss. $550.00

Made in Bohemia, circa 1875, and blown of leadless glass, this vase measures 10" in height and has a balustroid-shaped lower body, collar foot rim, and elongated neck which flares to a 3¾" open top. Decorated with cold enamel painting with stylized wheat, leaves, berries, and bluebells, all accented with gold on an acid-matte satin ground, the vase has the original seal comprised of a round metal plug covered by a glass disc, cemented into the pontil scar underfoot. Condition is excellent with very minor wear and no loss of silvering. $450.00

Bohemia, circa 1870 – 1880, this blown, non-flint glass vase has a tapered, cylindrical body and measures 8" tall. Decorated with a vapor-acid satin-matte ground, the vase features translucent cold painting of a bird with bright, multi-colored plumage resting on a branch along with bright orange and yellow blossoms. There are narrow bands of blue painted around the top and bottom rim, and around the base body collar, stem knop, and foot rim. The vase interior shows a bright, gold-washed stain, and the interior is narrow and deep. Original seal underfoot, with lead or metal round plug covered with glass disc. Some minor wear of the blue band painting, silvering shows no loss. $325.00

Made in Bohemia, circa 1880, this vase measures 6¼" tall. Blown of non-flint glass and light in weight, with a rare and unusual hand-painted parrot, stylized flowers and leaves, accented by gold enamel work and thin blue lines around the top and bottom cylindrical body. The seal consists of a plain round glass disc cemented underfoot. No significant wear, nor loss of silvering. $450.00

Made in Bohemia, circa 1870 – 1880, blown, non-flint glass, measuring 9¼" tall. Blown in reverse-baluster shape with a rounded foot and elongated, flared neck. Hand painted on acid-vapor satin matte ground, with a floral garland, gold butterfly, and other gold enamel accents. The vase has the original lead plug and glass disc underfoot. There is minor wear on the surface enameling, and the silvering is spotty underfoot with minor patch loss visible through foot rim. $225.00

Bohemian or German made, circa 1900 – 1920, made of non-lead glass, blown or possibly blown-molded. The vase measures 6¼" in height with tapered, elongated trumpet-shaped body and geometric concentric painted blue rings in an art deco style. Original metal and glass disc seal, showing silver flaking loss on foot, minor wear to paint. $125.00

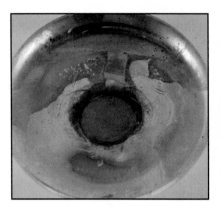

Made in Bohemia around 1870, this grand matched pair of vases features a well-executed floral, fern, and leaf motif in cold enamel painting along with applied gold enamel accents on a satin acid-vapor matte ground. Measuring 10¼" tall, the vases have an ovoid-shaped body rising to a tapered flared neck on the upper third of the piece, with a bottom collar, and round spread foot below the body. Both have their original metal seal and glass disc closure, and show some minor thinning to the silvering on the foot. $900.00 pair

Bohemia, circa 1880, this non-flint glass vase, blown in a cylindrical shape, measures 8¼" tall. Decorated with a rich ruby intaglio plate flashing with palm trees, ferns, and flora. Original metal plug and glass seal underfoot, with all silvering intact and no wear. $475.00

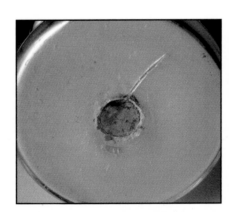

Made in Bohemia circa 1870 – 1880, this vase measures 10¼" tall. Blown and molded non-flint glass with fine rib panels, a gold-washed interior and decorated with the granulate white etching technique consisting of fine-detailed ferns, large palm leaves, and narrow bands. The original lead disc is cemented under foot in the rough pontil scar. No glass disc cover. No loss of silvering, no wear to surface decoration. $425.00

Bohemia, circa 1860 – 1870, blown lead glass with an unusual and rare serpentine shape measuring 10¼" tall and is heavy for its size. Features granulate crystal etching with grapes, grape leaves, grape vines, tendrils, and birds all over the body, with grape motif designs around the top foot. The surface granulate is lustrous in bright light. The interior is gold washed with a deep, rich glowing stain, and it has its original metal glass plug and glass disc cemented in the polished pontil hole underfoot. No silvering loss, no surface wear. Quality workmanship, could be unmarked Wolf or Scheinhost. $1,250.00

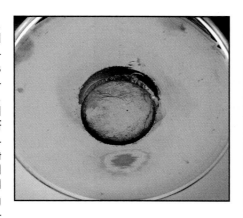

Made in Bohemia circa 1880, this non-flint glass, blown and molded vase measures 10½" tall and has a bright, gold washed interior. Featuring large patterned granulate crystal etched work with palm trees, leaves, vines, and bands, the piece has multiple molded vertical panels all around the tapered cylindrical body. Retains its original lead round plug and glass disc. No loss of silvering or wear. $475.00

Bohemia, circa 1870 – 1880, blown, non-lead glass, measures 11" tall, and decorated with applied granulate crystal etch work consisting of palm trees, ferns, leaves, vines, and a tropical bird. Has a rich, gold washed interior, and unusually tall cylindrical shape on tall foot. There is additional stylized leaf and vine etching on top of the foot, and it has the original metal plug and glass disc in place underfoot in the rough pontil scar. With only slight silvering spottiness on lower foot, and no wear, the vase is in excellent condition. $450.00

Bohemia, circa 1880, blown, non-flint glass, measuring 10¾" tall, in an unusual tapered chalice shape with etched palm trees, leaves, ferns, a bird, additional etched bands and gold washed interior. Silvering is exceptionally bright, with very minor wear to some of the etched surfaces. $475.00

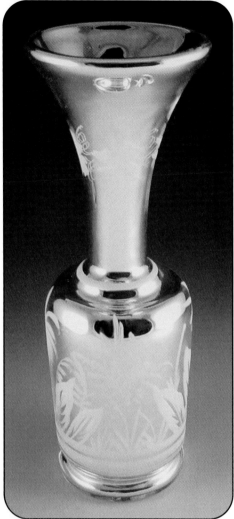

Made in Bohemia, circa 1880 – 1890, blown of non-lead glass, and measuring 8" tall, the vase has an unusually elongated neck, gold washed interior, and is granulate-etched with a combination of grape leaves and vines near the top of the flared neck. The pattern shows birds, palm trees, and leaves applied to the rounded, cylindrical lower body. The vase has a collar foot rim and its original metal plug and glass disc, and also bearing remnants of a rectangular paper label marked W.C.C. Moultin (?) 164 Essex Street, Salem, MASS. Possible retail firm? Silvering intact with no loss, no wear, and unusual label. $350.00

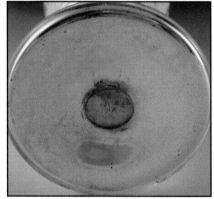

Bohemia, circa 1870 – 1880, blown non-lead glass, and measuring about 10½" tall, this vase is decorated with granulate powder etching, consisting of stylized ferns, leaves, and palm trees. The body is a reverse ovoid baluster shape, has a brilliant gold washed interior, with a narrow and deep opening. With its original lead plug under glass disc. No loss of silvering, there is only some minor wear. $425.00

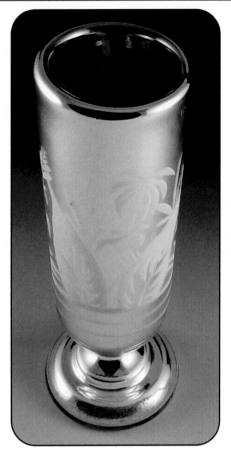

Bohemia, circa 1870 – 1880, blown of non-flint glass, this vase measures 8½" tall, with a straight-sided cylindrical shape, gold washed interior, and decorated with granulate etched stylized palm trees, leaves, and bands. There is slight discoloration of silvering and spottiness to the top of the round foot, and minor wear to parts of the etched areas. $250.00

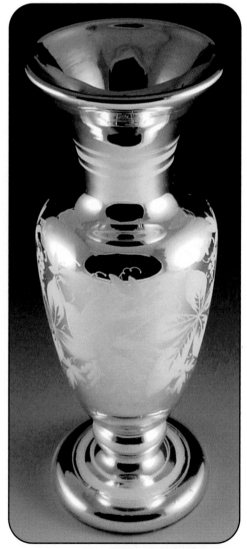

Made in Bohemia circa 1870 – 1880, non-lead glass, measures 10" tall, blown, reverse-baluster shape with turned foot and round base. With a rich, bright gold-washed interior and intricate, detailed granulate crystal white etch work featuring large leaves, bunches of grapes, grape leaves, vines, curling tendrils, and several large birds perched on branches. No loss of silvering, color is bright chrome, and minor etch wear on body. Original silver colored cardboard seal with glass disc cemented underfoot in the rough-edged pontil scar, the vase is of better quality. $450.00

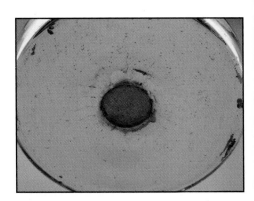

Bohemia, circa 1870 – 1880, blown and tooled non-lead glass, measures 8" tall, with etched ferns, palm trees, leaves, and bands, gold washed interior, which is unusually deep and narrow. The vase has a well-balanced body and ample round foot and neck. No silvering loss, and a minor surface indentation blemish done at time of manufacturing. The vase retains its original metal wafer seal and glass disc cemented loosely in pontil scar underfoot. $300.00

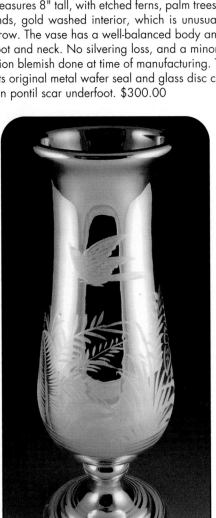

Made in Bohemia circa 1870 – 1880, blown non-flint glass, rounded baluster form, flares at neck rim, measures 10¾" tall. Decorated with light white crystal granulate etching showing finely detailed leaves, ferns, and wild grasses with a tall palm tree on one side and a bird in flight on the other side. The vase has a lustrous gold-washed interior, which is deep and ample. Retains its original round metal plug and glass disc cemented under-foot. Silvering shows no loss, very bright mirror chrome, and minor wear of granulate etching in areas. $375.00

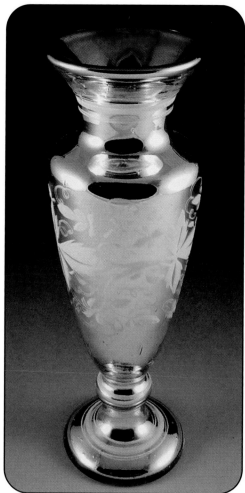

Made in Bohemia circa 1880, of fine grade soda-lime crystal, free blown, and measuring 9" tall. The vase is expertly decorated with white crystal granulate etching in a detailed, "vintage" pattern all around the reverse balustroid shape. It has the original lead plug and glass disc underfoot. No loss of silvering nor wear to any of the etch work. The interior is narrow, deep, and brightly gold washed. $350.00

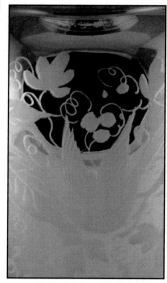

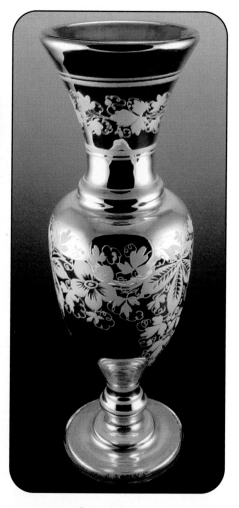

Made in Bohemia circa 1870, this vase is unusually tall measuring 14" high, and is blown in a reverse baluster shape with an elongated neck and large rounded foot. The patter is expert and intricate, consisting of an applied granulate white etched pattern with graceful meandering vines, curly tendrils, stylized blossoms, and grape leaves arranged garland style around the body. Further bands of granulate etching highlight the neck and foot rim. The vase has a light toned gold washed interior stain and a flared top opening. Original metal plug and glass disc underfoot cemented into smooth pontil scar. There is some spottiness and minor flaking loss of the silvering on the foot. $575.00

Made in Bohemia circa 1860 – 1870, blown of non-lead glass with a wide flat collar reverse baluster body, and measuring 10" tall with a short, flared neck and collar stem, this bold styled vase has a deep-toned gold washed interior and is decorated with fine white granulate etch work consisting of stylized palm trees, large leaves, wild grass, and feathered ferns, along with several birds in flight. The silvering is a bright chrome mirror finish, showing no loss, and only very minor wear on the etch work. The original silver colored glass disc is cemented in the semi-polished pontil scar underfoot. $450.00

Made in Bohemia circa 1870 – 1880, and blown of quality crystal glass into a large, reverse baluster urn shape with a short neck, but flaring to a wide 4½" open top and measuring a magnificent 12" tall. The vase is decorated with a series of concentric etched granulate bands around top collar and large, vertically oriented stylized leaves, ferns, and flowers, with a bird in flight on one side. The interior is rather shallow, and has a rich, deep amber-colored stain, which is highly lustrous. The surface is brilliant mirror chrome silver without loss, no wear. Unusual shape and rare size. $950.00

Made in Bohemia circa 1870, blown-molded light lead glass, measuring 14½" in height, with granulate etched work to elongated neck and lower body under molded ring configurations. The vase has a gold washed interior and features its original metal plug and glass disc cemented in the rough pontil scar underfoot. There is no loss of silvering, no wear to the surface decorations, but shows a mold line crease on side done during manufacturing. The vase is unusual in size and shape. $850.00

Maker unknown, possibly Bohemia, made for export to the United States, this unusual vase, made of non-lead glass and blown-molded, measures 10¾" tall. With a flared trumpet neck, round collar, and gradual cylindrical shape, the piece has a simple collar bottom, knop-footed stem, and round, ample foot. Featuring an acid-vapor satin-matte ground, the vase is decorated with a rare, applied decal showing the United States bald eagle, a 13-star American flag stylized shield, and cartouche scrolls in gold in an emblem that shows the dates 1776 and 1876, and marked for the 1876 Philadelphia Centennial Exposition, probably as a souvenir. There is wear to the silvering and wear loss to the painted decal. The open pontil hole has been covered with wax, original seal is lost, and flake loss to the round foot. A Centennial souvenir is rare to find and the size is unusual. $750.00

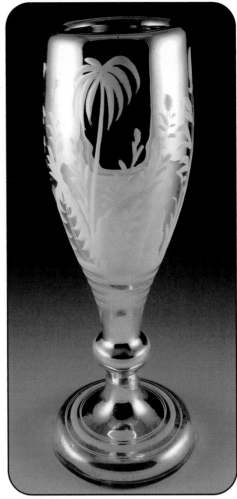

Made in Bohemia, blown and marvered of non-flint glass, circa 1870 – 1880, this 9½" tall vase has an elongated tapered flute shape, long knopped stem, and a round foot. It is decorated with fine applied granulate etch work consisting of palm trees, ferns and stylized leaves. With a deep toned gold-washed bowl. The silvering color is bright mirror chrome, with a very minor haze patch on the top of the foot. Original metal plug and glass disc over the rough pontil scar underfoot. $425.00

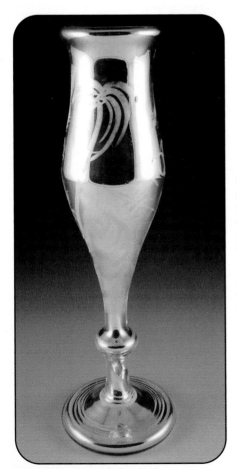

Made in Bohemia or Germany circa 1870 – 1880, of non-flint glass, and free-blown in an unusual floriform shape, this bud vase measures 9½" tall. It is decorated with a fine granulate application technique with a motif consisting of a bird in flight, palm trees, vines, leaves, and bands. There is one round knop to the long stem. The piece retains its original metal or card-board round closure, and has a glass disc cemented into the smoothed pontil scar underfoot. There is no loss of silvering, but there are typical bubbles consistent with soda-lime glass, and the vase is slightly tilted, done during manufacturing. $250.00

Bohemia circa 1870 – 1880, this blown, baluster ovoid-shaped vase has a tapered neck, gold washed interior, and a small, round foot. The vase measures 8" high and is decorated with white powder granulate ferns in several styles with leaves, palm trees, and circular bands. It retains the original lead or metal plug and glass disc, which is cemented into the smoothed pontil scar underfoot. No silvering loss, and surface is bright mirror chrome. $325.00

Made in Bohemia circa 1860 – 1870, and free blown of heavy non-lead glass, this marvelous pair of crystal silvered glass vases has a reverse baluster shape, an elongated neck flaring up to a wide rim, and a deep, amber gold-washed interior. The vases are decorated with a fine, white granulate crystal etch work consisting of well-executed vine and teardrop bands on the neck, berries and vines in double band around the top of the rounded body, draped leaf festoons, birds and flower bouquets, and thin pencil-line bands applied to the graduated short stems ending in a large, rounded foot. The silvering is a bright chrome color, with an exceptional brilliant mirror polish, no loss of silvering. Original metal plugs and round glass discs underfoot. $1,200.00 pair

Matched pair of quality made vases, crafted in Bohemia circa 1860 – 1870, free-blown of Bohemian crystal, with graceful, tulip bodies that flare to a pan opening, and measuring 10" tall. Each vase has a deep, amber-hued colored gold-washed interior and is expertly decorated with the applied granulate crystal etch technique in an intricate and unusual pattern consisting of stylized filigree chains around the rim, with double-lined band containing solid etch dotting. Further embellishments consist of curly vines, berries, branch-es, and leaves with two birds perched among the foliage in panels around the body, with a repeated band design applied to the lower tapered portion of the body. Additional vintage grapevine leaves and tendrils decorate the top surface of the large, rounded foot.

The condition of this fine pair of vases is extra fine with bright, mirror silver surface color and copper rich stained interiors. Both vases retain their original lead plugs and glass discs, which are cemented in each unusually large polished pontil opening. $1,750.00 pair

Monumental and rare matched pair of blown Bohemian crystal non-lead glass vases, made in Bohemia circa 1860 – 1870, measuring 14½" tall. With a round, balustroid teardrop shape and a long tapered neck flar-ing to wide trumpet opening, each vase has a bright gold-washed interior and is decorated with fine white dense crystal granulate etch work featuring tall cranes, large palm trees, styl-ized ferns, leaves, and pencil-thin bands around the lower por-tion of the bulbous body, and on both the upper and lower round foot. The vases have their original metal plugs and glass discs fitted into smoothed pontil scars underfoot, and both seals are large for their size. The silvering is bright, rich chrome, and all intact with some very minor cloudiness on the foot of one vase. $2,200.00 pair

Made in England circa 1850 – 1855, this very rare matched pair of blown silvered lead glass vases, measuring approximately 9" tall, are cased or plated with a clear layer of bright emerald green glass, expertly cut to silvered, and marked E. Varnish & Co., Patent, London. Blown in an ovoid shape with a collar neck flaring to a deeply mitered cut rim, the design contains a cut arched lattice and oval patterning, a cut oval and faceted stem with spiral navettes around large round, spread base. Both vases retain their embossed metal plugs, with E. Varnish & Co. Patent London, under clear glass discs, which were ground to fit into the polished pontil openings. In addition to the marked seals, there are diamond stylus etched numbers including "7349" under foot and "836" on outside of the glass disc and adjacent to the disc on one vase, and "7342" and "826" on the other vase, suggesting the pieces were numbered to match the seals to the vases, and possibly, the vases to each other, although the numbers are not exactly sequential. Of note, is that one vase is about one quarter inch taller than the other. These rare matched vases are in exquisite, original condition without any loss of silvering, and are exceptionally brilliant and well styled. $16,000.00 pair

Jungle Vase

Made in Bohemia and possibly unique, this monumental blown Bohemian glass vase, measuring 19½" tall, has a reverse ovoid baluster shape, elongated neck, and a wide, trumpet-shaped top rim. The body is decorated with an exceedingly rare and unusual applied granulate crystal technique, in what can be best described as jungle scenes of a male lion vanquishing a stylized snake on one side, and a tiger poised on the prowl on the other side. There are  ferns, palm trees, palmetto leaves, and birds all around the animals and between the lion and tiger. The neck of the vase has a fine and intricate drape pattern consisting of stylized grape leaves and vines, and the foot has an intricate dotted and filigree chain all around. This extraordinary vase was possibly made as a showroom piece to display the quality and variety of designs available. The vase has a short interior, with a bright gold wash, and was probably never made to hold flowers or water. The original seal, consisting of a grayish metal plug and glass disc, measures 1½" in diameter, and is an unusual size. The silvering is intact with some minor spotting around the top rim edge and foot. $5,500.00

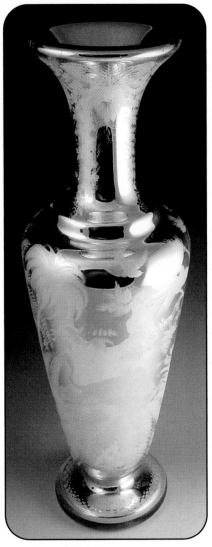

Chinese Chinoserie Vase

Monumental and important "Chinese Chinoserie" blown Bohemian crystal glass vase measuring 16½" tall, and attributed to the firm of Hugo Wolf, Bohemia, circa 1870 – 1880. The vase is decorated with a number of extraordinarily well-painted Mandarin figures, showing a high degree of artistic merit, along with granulate frosted peonies, a pagoda, flying crane, and other flowery motifs. The top of the vase is embellished with cabochon "diamond" cut applied glass "jewels" which are set within finely detailed filigree etched cartouche ovals. The shape of the body is a simple reverse oval baluster with a short collar round foot and a plain, urn shaped neck. The flowers show expert shading, using translucent bright, jewel-tone hues. Likely made as a showpiece to display the workmanship of the artists, there is only one other vase known to exist. The vase retains its original seal, with the impressed "HW" for Hugo Wolf, Iglau, Bohemia, under glass seal, cemented in the smooth-polished pontil scar, which is large for its size. The silvering is intact, and the bright, mirror surface shows no loss and no wear. $5,000.00

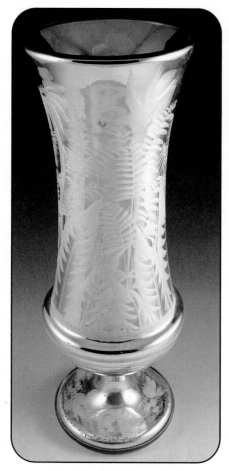

Monumental single blown Bohemian glass vase circa 1870 – 1880, flared cylindrical body, collar base, footed stem, large, round foot, and heavy for its size. The vase measures 12" tall and has a deep amber colored gold washed interior, and the body is decorated with granulate crystal etch work in a dense foliage pattern consisting of ferns, leaves, palm trees, and two birds, one in flight, the other perched on a branch. The top of the rounded foot has additional granulated etch work in the vintage pattern, showing grapes, tendrils, and grape-leaves around the surface. The vase retains its original metal plug and glass disc cemented into the smoothed pontil scar, the silvering is intact, but there is some very minor clouded spottiness to the upper foot area. $1,150.00

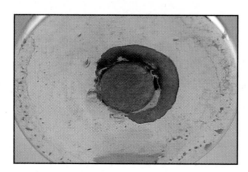

Matched pair of non-lead Bohemian glass vases, measuring 6¼" tall, which were free blown and marvered into an ovoid shape with a flared trumpet neck and collar stem, ending in a round, spread foot. Featuring an acid-vapor satin matte finish to most of the neck and body surface, the vases have an intricate Byzantine or Gothic inspired design, consisting of applied gold enamel dots, teardrops, and banding, together with black enamel pencil line scroll work, white floral garlands, and blossoms accented with ruby red highlights. They are light in weight and retain their original metal plugs and round glass discs underfoot. There is some patch loss to the silvering on one vase, and minor spotting on the other. $600.00 pair

Unusual sized blown and possibly molded non-lead glass vase, measuring about 4¼" tall, and made in Bohemia or Germany circa 1880 – 1890, probably for export. The vase features hand-painted orange blossoms and green leaves around the middle, in a simple, unsophisticated style that could have been done after manufacture. The top rim is slightly gold-washed stained, and the form is a chunky collared urn shape with a squat stem and round lower foot. The original metal plug and glass disc is in place under-foot. Small flake loss to the silvering and pigment loss to some areas of the painted flowers. $145.00

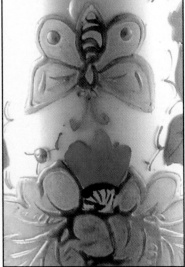

Bohemian blown and marvered or possibly blown molded non-lead glass vase, circa 1870 – 1880, with allover acid-vapor satin matte ground, featuring opaque painted flowers in blue, orange, and yellow, together with shaded green leaves and painted ebony branches accented with applied gold enamel dots. A large, stylized butterfly and pair of large leaves in gold are centered on the lower body, and the design is on only one side of the vase. There are three pencil bands in blue. The piece retains its original metal plug and glass disc cemented underfoot. There is no loss of silver-ing and only minor surface wear to the enamel and painted areas. $450.00

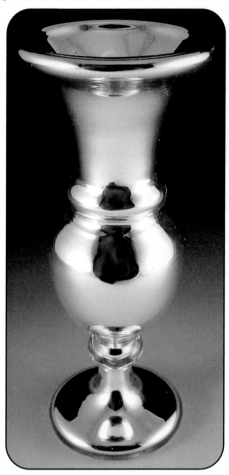

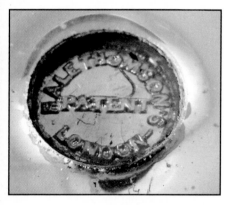

Hale Thompson's Patent London
English blown lead or flint glass plain mirror vase, circa 1850, measuring 7½" tall, with a rounded body, elongated neck gradually pulled to a large, flared trumpet top, knopped lower stem, and round foot. The piece is heavy for its size and has the original closure, consisting of a metal plug stamped, Hale Thomson's Patent London, covered with round glass disc, ground to fit the polished round pontil scar, cemented into place. Silvering is bright and chrome mirror with no loss of silvering and in excellent near original condition. $875.00

Blown, non-lead glass made in Bohemia, circa 1870, measuring 6¾" tall, with a round body, collar-based elongated trumpet-shaped neck and flared rim, on flat collar foot. Applied granulate etch work with Gothic banding around the neck, and birds, grape leaves, and vines to the lower body. There is some patch silvering loss to the body, with thin and spotted silvering to foot, and patch loss to the top rim. Original metal plug and glass disc underfoot. $175.00

Made in Bohemia, circa 1870 – 1880, this non-lead blown glass vase has a collar notch neck, short flared rim, long ovoid body, knopped lower stem, and a round foot. The piece has a medium toned gold-washed interior, with narrow, deep well, and is decorated with the applied granulate crystal technique in a pattern featuring ferns, leaves, palm trees, and wild grasses, together with concentric banding to the lower body and top of the round foot. Original metal plug and glass disc underfoot. The silvering is chrome mirror and bright, with some minor spot wear to the outer foot rim. $225.00

A pair of matched blown non-lead glass vases, made in Bohemia circa 1860 – 1870, measuring 8¾" tall, have reverse baluster ovoid body shapes and trumpet shaped necks flaring out to a large rim. The vases have bright, gold washed interiors, and are decorated with applied granulate crystal powder etching, in a fine and intricate pattern consisting of curly tendrils and leaves on the body and banding on the neck, stem, and foot. Original lead plugs and glass discs. The silvering is bright mirror chrome, with some spot loss under the foot on one vase. $950.00 pair

Blown molded and made of non-lead glass, this vase, measuring 6¼" tall, was made in Germany or Bohemia circa 1880. It features a hand-painted bird with leaves and palms in a rustic, naïve style. The vase retains the original metal plug and glass disc, although the seal is slightly loose and pushed into the pontil scar. There is some patch loss and spottiness on the surface with wear and staining to paint pigments. $125.00

This 12¼" blown non-lead glass vase, made in Germany or Bohemia circa 1880, has a classic reverse baluster shape with a flared trumpet neck and is hand painted in a naïve style with a stylized cream and peach colored center rose and leaves. The vase has some spottiness in the silvering at the rim and foot, and wear to the surface paint pigments with some noticeable paint loss. $425.00

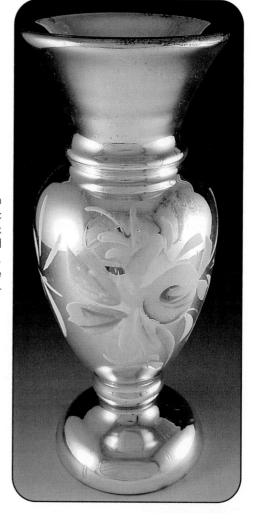

Blown non-lead 9" Bohemian glass vase, made circa 1860 – 1880, with a reverse baluster body, elongated trumpet neck, gold washed interior, and decorated with granulate crystal application etching in an intricate pattern consisting of grape leaves, vines, and long, curling tendrils all around the body. There is a series of bands in varying widths on top of the rounded foot. The piece retains its original foil seal and glass disc cemented into the roughened pontil scar underfoot. The silvering has slight misty hazing on the inside neck and on a small area on the body of the vase. $325.00

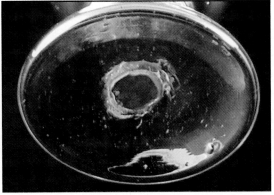

Blown, non-flint 8½" glass vase, made in Bohemia circa 1860 – 1880, with a tapered ovoid body, gold washed interior, and decorated with stylized ferns, leaves, and flowers in the applied dense crystal granulate etching technique. The piece has its original lead seal and glass disc fitted into the rough pontil scar underfoot. There is thinning, spotting, and silvering loss to the top of the vase. $225.00

Blown, non-lead glass vase, made in Bohemia or Germany circa 1860 – 1880, and measuring 3½" tall, an unusual size. The vase has a bright gold washed interior, and is decorated with shallow engraving in a naïve "vintage" pattern. The piece retains its original lead seal and disc, which is large, compared to the size. Silvering is intact. $125.00

Blown, molded non-flint glass vase, made in Bohemia circa 1870 – 1890, measuring 6¼" tall, with a long rounded body, on foot, and decorated with a ground of acid-vapor satin matting, cold enamel application, and pink, green, and gold paint in a Byzantine design consisting of a center cartouches, bands, and swags, together with flowers, and outlined in translucent color. The piece is lightweight for its size, and retains its original foil and glass disc seal cemented into the rough pontil scar underfoot. There is some minor thinning, spottiness and patch loss to the lower stem and foot. $300.00

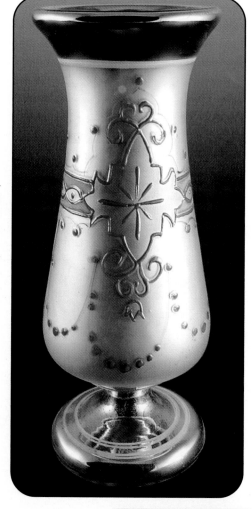

Blown, molded non-lead glass vase, made in Bohemia circa 1870 – 1890, measuring 10" tall, with an ovoid baluster shape, decorated with vapor-acid satin matte ground, and hand painted with a naïve floral and leaf design in bright, primary colors. There is a short stem and round foot. The piece has its original lead seal cemented into the rough pontil scar underfoot. There is some thinning of the silvering and spottiness to the top of the foot, and the vase is very light in weight for its size. $275.00

Blown flint glass vase on foot, made in the United States circa 1855 – 1870, probably Dithridge or another Pennsylvania maker, measuring 9" tall, featuring a straight-sided long tulip-shaped bowl and a round, balustroid knop spread to a large, rounded foot. The piece is very heavy for its size, and the color is deep dark mirror chrome. The vase has an amalgam metal seal in the rough pontil scar underfoot. $650.00

Rare pair of blown flint glass vases on foot, made in the United States circa 1855 – 1870, probably New England area glass-maker, possibly Boston & Sandwich or the Boston Silver Glass Company. The pair is wheel engraved in the "vintage" pattern, consisting of grapes, leaves, curling tendrils, and vines. There are oval knops under the long, tulipshaped bowls, which are spread to a large, round foot. The pair has their original cork seal inserted into the rough pontil scar underfoot. The color is bright mirror chrome, and the silvering is intact to all surfaces. $1,500.00 pair

Blown, cased, and cut to silver lead glass vase, made in England circa 1849 – 1855, measuring 7¼" tall, with a long, trumpet neck, turned collar knop, balustroid body, and medium stem spread to a round foot. The bright emerald green casing is cut away in circles around the neck, and the body is cut in a geometric chevron pattern. The stem is cut with elongated ovals, and the foot is richly cut with navettes around the outer rim. The vase retains its original metal seal, stamped "Thomson Patent London" and covered with a circular glass disc sealed into the polished pontil scar underfoot. $2,500.00

Blown and molded non-flint 10½" tall glass vase on pedestal, made in Germany or Bohemia circa 1870 – 1890, with a large, deep tulip-form body and unusual molded bell-shaped platform foot. The glass has bubbles and striations. The vase retains its original metal seal and glass disc cemented into the rough pontil scar underfoot. The color is bright chrome silver. $225.00

Blown and molded lead glass vase, measuring 10¾" tall, possibly late American or Continental, featuring cold paint white enamel decorations with grape clusters, curling tendrils, vines, and leaves. The large urn-shaped body is slightly tapered, and the foot is deep and turned. The piece has a cork in place in the rough pontil scar, which is not original. The color is deep chrome silver. $250.00

Blown molded non-flint glass vase, measuring 12" tall, made in Bohemia or Germany circa 1870 – 1890, with a tapered, cylindrical body, short stem, and round foot. The vase is decorated with hand-painted bird, flowers, and leaves in a naïve style, against an acidvapor satin matte ground and the interior is light gold washed. The vase has its original metal seal and glass disc inserted into the rough pontil hole underfoot. Unusual size. $500.00

Silvered mercury glass proved to be an important medium for the creation of various types of drinking vessels which are represented in all manner of form and decoration.

A goblet, by definition, is simply a drinking glass with a large bowl and a stemmed foot. Goblets were made in many sizes, often with varying bowl forms, and can found with a wide variety of stylistic variations in the actual stem and foot. The most common bowl forms used in footed silvered glass goblets are the bell shape, which is rounded and looks like an inverted bell, and the bucket form, which has a basic flared cylindrical shape, but tapers to a flat, almost square bottom. Beakers, which are very similar, also have a cylindrical shape with a flared mouth, but are usually flat with a collar base or have a much shorter stem when compared to a goblet.

Because of the double-walled glass layers, the stems of silvered glass goblets are thicker and shorter as compared to those made of other types of glass. Although the baluster or reverse baluster shapes are sometimes found, the stems of silvered glass goblets are generally plain, serving to attach the bowl to the circular foot. A rare stem form, found on the English pieces, involved cut or faceted work. Other goblet stems have knops.

Knops are embellishments, usually round or oval, which protrude out on the stem of the glass. Some silvered glass goblets have flattened or globular knops equidistant from bowl to foot, or ball and collar knops right under the bowl. Beakers often have annular or ring-shaped knops formed in various locations on the short stem.

Silvered glass goblets and beakers vary in size, and examples illustrated in this chapter range from just about four to over ten inches tall. The average height for a goblet is six inches while beakers are usually wider and shorter, and measure about five inches tall. The ratio of height to rim size is less on a beaker and greater on a goblet. Goblets have a more formal appearance, while beakers appear more utilitarian.

A mug is a drinking vessel with a handle, cylindrical shape, and a circular rim that rests on a flat base. Mercury glass mugs are generally much smaller in size when compared to mugs of other materials, and average only about four inches tall.

The pokal, a form that is German in origin, is shaped like a goblet, although usually larger, and has a cover, or lid that is topped with a finial. This special type of large goblet was passed around from person to person for the purpose of drinking a toast during ceremonious occasions. Covered pokals are rare to find, and were probably made as presentation pieces. The one example illustrated in this chapter stands just about fourteen inches tall, from the base of the foot to the top of the finial!

The decorative techniques applied to silvered glass vessels are almost as varied as those used on vases. Goblet forms, which are generally American or English, were made plain, wheel-engraved, or cased and cut to silver. The beakers and mugs, usually Bohemian or German in origin, were decorated with other techniques, including applied granulate crystal etching, surface engraving, or enamel and paint work on an acid-treated satin matte background. The Bohemian or German-made beakers and goblets more often have gold-washed interiors when compared to the other makers. Although English pieces can be found with the gold interiors, American made silvered mercury glass never has a gold interior.

In terms of production, beakers, goblets, and other drinking vessels were made in great quantities, second only in volume to vases.

With respect to relative age and years of production, goblets made in the United States were produced for about twenty years beginning around the early 1850s and lasting into the 1870s. English pieces were produced only for about five years, beginning in 1849 and lasting to around 1854. However, the drinking vessels made in Bohemia and Germany, including beakers, goblets, and mugs, were made for a longer period of time, beginning from around 1850 and continuing through the first decade of the twentieth century.

The value of each goblet, beaker, or mug, as with other forms, depends on the quality of workmanship, condition of the piece, as well as its rarity, which is always relative to the years of production and the rates of survival. For that reason, drinking vessels made in Bohemia are generally priced within the reach of the average collector, while English-made items are expensive to acquire. Goblets made in the United States, whether plain or engraved, form the middle of the market, although, when part of a matched set of presentation of specialized sets, can command much higher prices.

Presentation pokal, made in Bohemia, 1870 – 1880, by the firm of Hugo Wolf, blown and molded of Bohemian crystal, measuring 10½" tall, with a large, funnel-shaped bowl on a tall stem, featuring a center knop, with honeycomb pattern faceting, and outlined with white enamel. Decorated in the Moorish taste with intricate interwoven, curvilinear designs including a stylized fleur-de-lis, using wax resist acid-etch work outlined in white enamel. It is probable that this piece was made with a matching lid that was lost. The bowl has a slightly flared rim, and the mouth measures 4¾" wide. The round foot measures 4" in diameter. The piece retains its original seal, including a metal disc stamped "HW" for Hugo Wolf, with a circular glass disc cover cemented into the polished pontil scar underfoot. Some minor spotting and cloudiness to foot, with patch silvering loss around seal area. $2,500.00

Blown, English-made lead glass goblet, measuring 9½" tall, circa 1850, cased or plated in rich cobalt blue cut to silver, and marked E. Varnish & Co., Patent England. The piece has a deep, round funnel-shaped bowl with a slight pan-shape top rim, and a cut and faceted baluster stem, with a double row of flat ovals cut on the top and edge of the bottom foot rim. The bowl has a cut surface pattern comprised of long ovals and arches with double-circle flat cuts where the long ovals connect around the bowl. The goblet retains its original seal, marked as above, with glass disc over stamped metal seal. Excellent condition with no silvering loss or damage. $6,000.00

Blown lead glass goblet, Bohemia, measures 7½" tall, made circa 1870 – 1880, with rare and unusual glass bead jewels in sapphire blue, ruby red, and emerald green applied on the surface to accent the intricate Byzantine design, made with applied crystal granulate etching, and consisting of arches, curvilinear bands, stylized blossoms and leaves, and trailing trellis motifs. The large, globular, cup-shaped bowl is deep and has an intense, gold-washed interior, and the surfaces are bright chrome silver. The stem has a double-ring knop adjacent to the bowl, and flows to a round foot. The piece has its original metal disc seal, covered with a glass disc, cemented into a polished pontil scar underfoot. $1,500.00

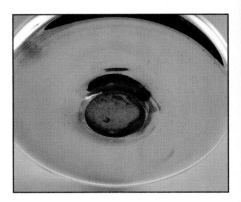

Footed beaker, blown of lead glass, made in Bohemia, circa 1870 – 1880, with rare and unusual glass jewels consisting of round, faceted emerald-green cabochons, sapphire blue beads, diamond-shaped appliqués in ruby red, and alternate clusters of grapes comprised of tiny glass beads alternating in pink and green around the surface. The jewels are accents interspersed in the white granulate etched pattern, consisting of an intricate array of garlands, medallions, and grape leaf and vine swags, with a fine filigree banding around the bottom of the tapered, deep funnel shaped-bowl, with fine grape and vine banding on the top of the foot, along the outer edge foot rim. The base of the bowl ends in a rounded protruded collar and has a short stem. The glass is brilliant mirror silver with no damage, in original condition. The piece retains its original seal, comprised of a metal disc stamped with the single letter "H," possibly associated with Hugo Wolf and is covered by a glass disc cemented into smooth and polished pontil scar underfoot. $1,500.00

Made in Bohemia or Germany, 1870 – 1880, of non-lead blown glass, this goblet, with a gold washed interior, modified bell-shaped bowl, and a short, waisted stem ending in round foot measures 5½" tall. Bowl has granulate-application etched white arched vines around the upper and lower bowl, with a center panel around the circumference showing birds in flight, grape leaves, and meandering vines. There is a series of graduated rings around bottom of stem. Retains its original metal plug and glass disc seal underfoot. Shows some minor hazing around top and bottom of foot. $250.00

Made in Bohemia, 1870 – 1880, this 5¾" tall footed beaker, of non-leaded blown glass, is decorated with acid-vapor satin matte ground, with hand-painted cold enamel flowers, leaves, and vines in shaded color, and accented with gold enamel beading in the center of the flowers. This goblet retains its original metal plug and glass disc over rough pontil scar underfoot. Interior is bright chrome silver. Minor patch loss of silvering to one area on upper foot. $350.00

Rare ruby flashed and surface wheel engraved to silver blown Bohemian glass footed beaker, measuring 5¾" tall, 1860 – 1870, with a straight cylindrical bowl and narrow stem ending in round foot. Engraved designs showing a band of circles around the top rim, band and geometric-form diamonds with Byzantine detail, panels, stylized fern chains and diamond and drop banding around bottom of bowl. With two more bands of circles engraved on the stem bottom and edge of the round foot. The goblet retains its original glass disc seal, which shows remnants of silvering on the interior. No wear to silvering and unusual design and color. $500.00

Blown and molded footed beaker, measuring 5½" tall, made in Bohemia, 1860 – 1870, of resonant non-lead glass, with granulate-applied etching consisting of birds perched on vines, with leaves, tendrils, and grapes all around the square-bottom urn bowl that flares out at rim. Has a bright gold-washed interior, and silvering is bright chrome and mirror surface with no loss. $275.00

Bohemian crystal formula blown glass footed goblet, 1870 – 1880, measuring 5¾" tall, with gold glass casing over tulip bowl, wheel engraved with large deer, trees, and forest scene. Rare and unusual combination of techniques, with a series of concentric stem and foot rings consisting of applied granulate etching resembling ice crystals. This goblet retains its original lead plug and round glass disc, applied in the polished and smoothed pontil scar underfoot. Unusual and rare engraving and color plating, with no loss of silvering. $525.00

Made in Bohemia or Germany, this blown glass goblet, 1860 – 1870, measuring 5½" tall, is decorated with a thin layer of ruby red flashing, with an intaglio stylized leaf and vine motif in silver, and accented with cold-painted white enamel. Collar ring knop at base of bell bowl, medium length stem, and round foot. The piece retains its original metal seal and glass disc cemented underfoot. The piece is heavy for its size and likely made of a Bohemian crystal formula. There is some spottiness to base of foot. $525.00

Blown lead glass made in Bohemia 1870 – 1880, this footed beaker, with a tapered cylindrical deep funnel-shaped bowl is decorated with rare and unusual glass bead appliqués in sapphire blue, emerald green, and ruby red that comprise the center of granulate applied crystal etching in a pattern of flowers, leaves, vines, and branches around the bowl. Crystal etching consisting of grape leaf and vine chain around foot, this piece measures 5" tall. Silvering is all intact in bright mirror-chrome. It retains its original metal seal and glass disc cemented into polished pontil scar underfoot. $750.00

Blown Bohemian footed beaker with a large, tapered cylindrical bowl, short stem, and round foot, 1870 – 1880, measuring 6¼" tall, and decorated with ruby flashing to silver, featuring birds in flight, stylized palm trees, ferns, leaves, and flowers accented with hand-painted cold white enameling. The beaker retains its original lead plug and glass disc cemented underfoot. The silvering is intact and bright mirror chrome. $675.00

Footed blown beaker, made in Germany or Bohemia, measuring 5¼" tall, 1870 – 1880, with a gold glass-plated band around the deep, round funnel-shaped bowl with shallow engraved Gothic arch banding, and a center leaf and vine band encircling the bowl. Stem is a reverse baluster ending in short stem and round foot. The piece retains its original metal and glass disc seal and there is some very light haze wear to the foot. $350.00

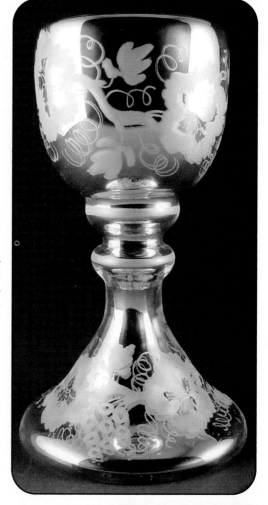

Unusual blown lead glass chalice, 1860 – 1870, measuring 7" tall, with deep gold washed interior and intricate granulate crystal application etching in a dense and complex "vintage" pattern all around the upper bowl and lower stem which flares out in a sweeping trumpet shape ending in a flat round foot. Silvering is intact and glass is unusually resonant with high bell tones. $425.00

Rare and unusual chalice with a large, deep and round bowl, a bright gold washed interior, a double layer knop under the bowl, and a tall stem, which flares to a round, flat foot. Made in Bohemia 1870 – 1880, the piece is decorated with coarse ground crystal granulate etching with a sparkling "ice" finish, in an intricate pattern consisting of scrolls, ribbons, arches, and enclosed cartouches accented with curvilinear whorls and stylized fleur-de-lis. The bottom stem has blue-tinted granulate appliqué work in a dense grape leaf and vine pattern encircling the piece. The piece is heavy, lead glass weight. Original metal plug and glass disc sealed into polished pontil scar underfoot. $1,500.00

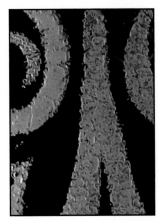

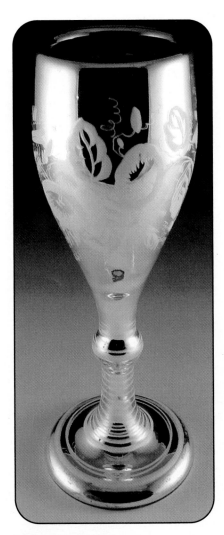

Blown Bohemian tall footed stem goblet, 1870 – 1880, measuring 9" tall, with a flute-shaped bowl, knopped stem, and round foot, decorated with applied granulate etching consisting of stylized flowers, leaves, tendrils, and vines with birds perched on branches around the bowl. There is a series of bands around the bottom of the stem and around the top round foot. The interior is deep copper-colored gold washed, and the silvering is all intact mirror chrome. Original glass disc painted silver on the inside cemented into the smoothed pontil scar underfoot. Unusual shape. $425.00

Footed beaker, made in Germany or Bohemia circa 1860 – 1870, measuring 5¼" tall, with bright gold washed interior, and granulate application etched "vintage" pattern all around the tapered cylindrical bowl on short stem. The piece has minor clouding, thinning, and spottiness to silvering on upper and lower surfaces of the foot. $225.00

Blown lead glass Bohemian footed beaker, circa 1870 – 1880, measuring 5" tall, with a flared bell bowl, short stem, and round foot. The piece has a bright gold washed interior, and the surface of the bowl is decorated with an intricate resist or template design, consisting of buildings, trees, and a woodland theme and a vintage grape vine chain around the top of the round foot, all done with applied granulate crystal "ice" technique. The piece retains its original glass disc, painted silver on the inside, cemented into a polished pontil scar underfoot. Silvering is intact with a bright mirror chrome color. $650.00

Important Bohemian blown lead glass footed beaker, circa 1860 – 1870, measuring 5¼" tall, with fine and intricate wheel engraved landmarks, in the Biedermeier style, showing the Sprudel, Karlsbad, which is a famous spa in Karlovy Vary, a town in the current Czech Republic, formerly Bohemia. The Sprudel spa was built around natural mineral springs, which contain waters thought to have curative or medicinal powers. The other points of interest include Markelbrunn, another spa, and others, which are all expertly engraved and captioned in German, within large longitudinal medallions. There are finely shaded grape leaves and curling tendrils above and below the oval cartouches and the piece shows a bright gold washed interior. The silvering is intact. The piece retains a silver foil seal and round glass disc cemented into the polished pontil area underfoot. $1,400.00

Blown of non-lead glass and made in Bohemia circa 1860 – 1870, this footed beaker, measuring 5¾" tall, is decorated with the granulate technique featuring birds perching on branches surrounded by stylized leaves and vines accented with curling tendrils. The inside is bright gold washed. The piece retains its original lead plug and glass disc cemented into the rough pontil scar underfoot. The silvering is intact and the granulate etch work is exceptionally detailed. $275.00

Mold blown and footed non-lead glass beaker, measuring 5¾" tall, was made in Bohemia circa 1870 – 1880, and decorated with intricate grape leaves, vines, and curling tendrils in a wide framed band around the bowl. The band frame consists of an arched Gothic band and single thin band done in the applied granulated powder technique. The piece is molded with soft contour vertical pillars or ribbing, which give the piece a scalloped look. With a wide flaring rim and a molded collar bowl base, the interior is bright gold-washed and the piece retains its original foil plug and glass disc secured into the rough pontil scar underfoot. The silvering is intact except for a small area at the bottom inside bowl. $300.00

Blown flint glass presentation goblet, made in the United States circa 1855 – 1870 and measuring 7¾" tall. This unusual piece was expertly wheel engraved with a cartouche shaped semi-wreath, stylized flowers, and a center bow, surrounding the name "Henry" in calligraphic script. Although speculative, this piece could have been engraved by either Henry Fillebrown or Henry Leighton, both of whom worked for the New England Glass Company. The bowl is deep bell-shaped, and the knop, baluster stem, and large rounded foot are graceful and balanced. The goblet was resealed with a cork, which is not original. There is some flaking of the silvering in patches on the top of the foot. The color is more yellow silver than chrome, possibly resulting from a loss of its original seal. $2,000.00

Blown Bohemian glass presentation pokal or covered goblet, circa 1860 – 1880, measuring 14" tall with cover, and decorated with crushed quartz granulate powder application in an intricate allover pattern consisting of scrolls, flowers, grapes, grape leaves, and vines, together with incised diamonds and Byzantine inspired cartouches, banding, and arch work against a brilliant bright chrome silver surface. The interior of the goblet is bright amber-colored gold washed, and the matching top has a large finial, which is decorated in granulate etch work to match. The bowl is a deep funnel shape, and the reverse baluster stem has a round platform bottom which spreads to a large, rounded foot. The goblet retains its original metal plug and glass disc, cemented into the polished pontil opening underfoot. The top has a cork in place, which is not original. The silvering is intact to the goblet, and the top has some minor hazing and patch loss to the under-surface. $5,200.00

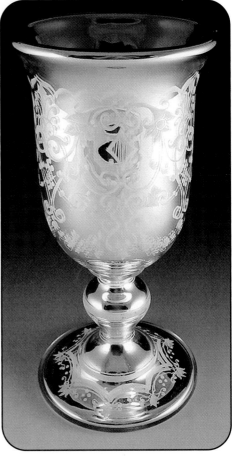

Blown flint glass goblet, made in the United States circa 1855 – 1870, and likely Boston & Sandwich Glass Company. The piece has a bucket bowl and short stem with a slight collar and measures 5¾" tall. Expertly engraved with a rare and unusual pattern consisting of a chain of dots around the upper rim, a leaf and flower chain, and a center motif with an open wreath and the initials "R.D." in old English script. There are tiny engraved stars all around the surface of the bowl and a curved scroll band around the outer edge of the round foot. Likely engraved by Carl Mattoni, the piece resembles others of provenance. The silvering is bright brilliant chrome and all intact. The piece retains its original cork in a rough pontil hole, with remnants of a red and silver paper seal. $2,000.00

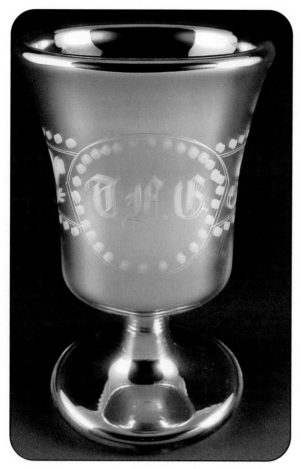

Blown flint glass goblet, made in the United States circa 1855 – 1875, Boston Silver Glass Company or Sandwich, measuring 6" tall, and engraved in an unusual pattern consisting of a center circle with three initials in old English, with a series of small dots encircling the initials and repeated above and below a center band with stylized blossoms all around the bucket shaped bowl. Color is bright mirror chrome with silvering intact. Retaining its original cork in a polished pontil scar underfoot. $950.00

Blown flint glass goblet, measuring 5" tall, made in the United States at the New England Glass Company, Cambridge, Massachusetts, and custom engraved with the initials and date: "S.C.M Dec: 25th 1863" within a finely detailed wreath containing intricate flowers and various shapes and forms of leaves, with a tied curling bow and, on the reverse, a bouquet consisting of spring and summer flowers showing botanically correct details. The bowl is bell shaped and the piece has a waisted stem and round foot. The goblet retains its original metal seal stamped "NEG Co." for the New England Glass Company, and a glass disc cemented into the polished pontil hole underfoot. Louis Vaupel could have done the fine and artistic engraving, as the fine work resembles much of his other work, although this is speculative without a signature. The silvered is slightly hazy on the inside of the bowl, and there is a minor fracture to the edge of the foot rim. $2,000.00

Pair of rare matching blown flint glass goblets, measuring 6½" tall, made in the United States, probably by Sandwich Glass or the Boston Silver Glass Company circa 1860, with custom engraved half wreath cartouches, a stylized center bow, and the initials '"C.J.P." in old English script. The bowls are round funnel shapes, with an unusual tall stem with a knop under the bowl, sweeping to a large, round foot. The silvering is deep mirror chrome and all intact. They retain their original cork in the rough and sharp edged pontil scar. Unusual to find pair. $3,200.00 pair

Blown flint glass footed goblet, made in the United States circa 1855 – 1870, probably New England area, possibly Boston Silver Glass Company or Boston & Sandwich Glass Co., Massachusetts, measuring 6" tall with a wide, larger rounded bucket bowl, short stem to spread round foot. The piece is engraved in fine detail featuring a stylized fern, flower, and leaf wreath cartouche, surrounding three initials: "A.W.C." in old English script. The goblet is heavy for its size, weighing one pound, and the color is dark chrome mirror silver. It retains its original cork seal in the rough pontil scar underfoot. $1,200.00

Blown flint glass goblet, made in the United States circa 1855 – 1870, probably Boston & Sandwich Glass Company, measuring 5¾" tall, with a finely detailed half wreath cartouche and the initials "M.A." in old English script. Likely custom made, as many initialed American pieces, the goblet has a deep bucket shaped bowl, short stem, and large rounded foot. The piece retains its original cork plug in the rough and sharp pontil scar underfoot, with remnants of a red and silver paper seal. Silvering is bright chrome and intact. $850.00

Blown flint glass goblet, made in the United States, possibly early New England Glass Company or the Boston & Sandwich Glass Company, circa 1855 – 1870, measuring 5¾" tall with a deep bucket-shaped bowl, and engraved in a Greek or Roman Key pattern all around the bowl. The engraving is deep and sharp to the touch, with a thin engraved band above and below the key. The piece is a bright silver chrome color, very heavy for its size, and retains its original cork plug in the rough and sharp pontil scar underfoot. No evidence of a paper seal. $750.00

Pair of blown flint glass goblets, circa 1855 – 1870, made in the United States, possibly Boston & Sandwich Glass Company or the Boston Silver Glass Company, measuring 7" tall with a knop and reverse baluster stem spreading to a large round foot. The pair is wheel engraved with a dense "vintage" pattern all around the deep bell bowl. The silvering is bright mirror chrome, all intact, and both retain their original cork seal in rough and sharp pontil scars underfoot. $1,500.00 pair

Blown flint glass goblet, circa 1855 – 1870, made in the United States, measuring 6¼" tall, possibly New England Glass Company, Cambridge, Massachusetts, with an unusual wide bell bowl and double-band framed Greek or Roman Key pattern. The stem is long and has a collar knop under the bowl ending with a round foot. Silvering is bright mirror and intact, and the piece has a nineteenth century paper label with a ink cartouche, no markings, appearing to cover a solid glass disc in the pontil polished scar underfoot. $850.00

Blown flint glass goblet, circa 1855 – 1870, made in the United States, probably Boston & Sandwich Glass Co., Massachusetts, measuring 5½" tall, with a round contoured modified bucket-shaped bowl which flares out at the top, and wheel engraved with the initials "T.S.S." in old English script enclosed in a floral and leaf wreath with a center bow. The piece has a short stem and very large round foot. There are interior scratches to the glass surface on the inside and the silvering is intact. The piece has a cork in the pontil scar with a layer of white wax, as found. $700.00

Blown flint glass goblet, circa 1860 – 1870, made in the United States, possibly by a Pennsylvania maker. The piece has a deep funnel-shaped bowl and a collar knop under the bowl narrowing to a long stem and spread round foot. The glass is lighter in weight than other American pieces of its size and has a high bell tone ring when tapped. The bowl is engraved with a left oriented Greek or Roman Key pattern with two incised lines above and below. The piece has a cork plug in a rough pontil scar with remnants of a dark gray paper seal. There are minor haze spots on the upper foot. $600.00

Large blown flint glass presentation goblet, made in the United States by the New England Glass Co., Cambridge, Massachusetts, circa 1855 – 1870, measuring 7" tall and wheel engraved in an unusual floral pattern which wraps around the entire surface of the deep funnel-shaped bowl, with a pan flared top rim. The engraving is of superior quality consisting of shaded petal flowers, lily-of-the-valley, and leaves in several sizes with botanically correct detail. The long stem is a true baluster, waisted at the bottom and the piece has a large round foot. The piece retains its original metal disc stamped with "NEG.Co." under a round glass disc cemented into place in the polished pontil scar underfoot. The silvering is bright warm metal color with some minor patch flaking underfoot. The piece is very heavy for its size weighing more than one pound. Possibly Louis Vaupel. $2,100.00

Blown flint glass goblet, made in the United States circa 1860 – 1880, Pennsylvania area, maker unknown, and measuring 5¾" tall. The piece has a classic bucket-shaped bowl flaring at the top rim, and a medium length stem spreading to a large round foot. The goblet is engraved with a small-scale berry, leaf, and curling tendrils pattern, and has three initials in old English script, which appear to be "F.O.T." The silvering is bright chrome color. There is a cork in the large rough pontil scar underfoot. There is some flaking loss in patches underfoot. $550.00

Pair of matched blown flint glass goblets, made in the United States, circa 1855 – 1870, Boston area, possibly Sandwich, and measuring 6" tall. The bowls are deep cylindrical modified bucket shapes, with a short, wide stem, and are wheel engraved in a wide and flowing "vintage" pattern all around the outside surface of each bowl. Both have a deep alto resonance when tapped and silvering is dark mirror chrome, some minor hazing around bottom of one stem at foot, with cork plugs intact in each rough and sharp pontil scar. $1,000.00 pair

Blown flint glass goblet, made in the United States, possibly Boston Silver Glass Company or Sandwich, circa 1855 – 1870, and measuring 5¾" tall. The goblet has a short wide stem and a deep, rounded bucket bowl. The piece is wheel engraved in an open "vintage" pattern all around the outside surface of the bowl. The color is bright mirror chrome silver. The piece retains its original cork seal in a rough and sharp pontil scar underfoot, showing remnants or a reddish paper seal. The piece has deep bell tone resonance and is lighter in weight than comparable goblets of the same size. $600.00

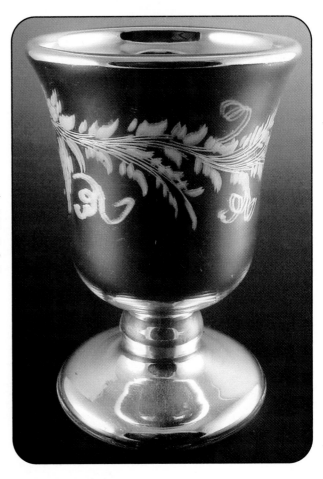

Blown flint glass goblet, made in the United States circa 1855 – 1870, possibly Pennsylvania, measuring 5½" tall, with an engraved thin leaved grape pattern all around the modified bucket bowl. The piece has a short and wide stem flowing to a large spread round foot. It has its original cork seal in the sharp edged pontil scar underfoot. Color is bright mirror chrome, with some minor hazing to the top of the foot. $525.00

Blown flint glass goblet, made in the United States circa 1855 – 1870, possibly Pennsylvania, measuring 6" tall with an unusually well-detailed vintage pattern showing shaded grape leaves with veins and fringe edging, grapevines, bunches of grapes, and curling tendrils all around the upper third of the bucket-shaped bowl. Medium stem flowing to a large round foot. It has its original cork seal in place in the unpolished pontil scar underfoot. The color is medium bright mirror chrome, and the silvering is intact. $750.00

Blown flint glass goblet, made in the United States circa 1855 – 1870, possibly Boston & Sandwich Glass Co., Massachusetts, measuring 5⅞" tall with a plain, deep chrome silver color, short stem, and large spread round foot. The piece is heavy for its size and retains its original cork seal in the unpolished pontil scar underfoot, with remnants of a round red and silver paper seal. $425.00

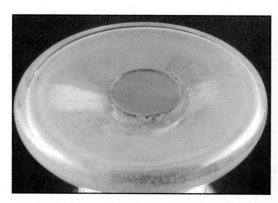

Blown and molded non-flint glass footed beaker, made in Bohemia circa 1860 – 1880, measuring 5½" tall, with a bright amber gold washed interior, and decorated in a fine, allover granulate-powder etching pattern consisting of large and small grape leaves and tight curling tendrils all around the outside of the waisted tulip-shaped bowl. The stem has a round collar under the bowl and a medium sized round foot. The piece retains its original metal plug and glass disc cemented into the unpolished pontil scar underfoot. The silvering is slightly cloudy on the rim of the foot with some loss underfoot. $275.00

Blown molded non-lead glass footed beaker, made in Bohemia circa 1860 – 1880, measuring 4¾" tall, with unusual gold staining to the outside surface of the bell-shaped bowl, showing resist-template leaves in gold intaglio against the applied white satin cold painting that is further accented with green leaves around the design. The piece shows bubbles and striations in the glass. It has its original lead or metal round seal and glass disc cemented into the unpolished pontil scar underfoot. $295.00

Blown molded non-flint glass footed beaker, measuring 3¾" tall, made in Bohemia circa 1860 – 1880, decorated with applied granulate powder etching in white, showing large grape leaves and tendrils encircling the outside of the bowl. The piece has a collar base at the bottom of the bowl and a short stem spread to a round platform pedestal on top of the large bottom foot. Both the interior and the collar knop are bright gold washed. The piece retains its original metal seal and glass disc in the unpolished pontil scar underfoot. Unusual size. $250.00

Blown non-flint glass footed beaker, made in Bohemia circa 1860 – 1880, measuring 4½" tall, decorated with the granulate-powder application technique in a dense, allover pattern consisting of leaves in various sizes and long, tightly curling tendrils all around the bowl. The piece has a medium stem ending a platform pedestal atop the round foot, and a bright amber interior gold wash. Original metal seal and glass disc cemented into the unpolished pontil scar underfoot. The beaker has a medium bright mirror chrome color and minor hazing underfoot. $275.00

Blown flint glass footed goblet, made in the United States circa 1855 – 1870, probably New England area, possibly Boston & Sandwich Glass Co., measuring 5¾" tall, and wheel engraved in the "vintage" pattern all around the rounded bucket-shaped bowl. The piece has a short stem spread to a large round foot.

It retains its original cork seal in the unpolished pontil scar and remnants of a red and silver paper seal. The color is deep mirror chrome and the silvering is intact. $575.00

Matched pair of blown flint glass presentation footed goblets, made in the United States, probably Dithridge or other Pennsylvania area maker, measuring 6¾" tall, with a deep tulip bowl and unusual true reverse baluster stems narrowing at base with a large, round spread foot. The surfaces are dark deep mirror chrome, without further embellishment. Both retain their original cork seal in the unpolished pontil scar underfoot, with one covered with additional metal amalgam seal. $1,200.00 pair

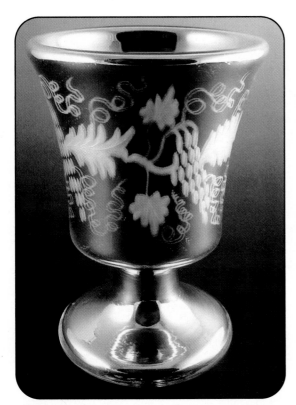

Blown flint glass footed goblet, made in the United States, measuring 5½" tall, probably Boston & Sandwich Glass Co. or the Boston Silver Glass Co., circa 1855 – 1870, with a well-defined vintage pattern filling the exterior surface of the bucket-shaped bowl all around the piece. Color is bright light chrome silver. The piece retains its original cork seal in the unpolished pontil scar. $550.00

Blown flint glass footed goblet, made in the United States, possibly Pennsylvania area, measuring 5⅞" tall, medium stem spreading to a large, round foot. The piece is engraved with the initials "F.G.M." in old English script and a meandering "vintage" pattern under the monogram and all around the piece. Color is bright mirror chrome. The piece has its original cork seal in a polished pontil scar underfoot. There is some minor having on the bottom of the stem and top of the foot. $625.00

Pair of matched blown flint glass footed goblets, made in the United States, probably the Boston & Sandwich Glass Co. or early New England Glass Co., each measuring 5¾" tall and wheel engraved with a Greek or Roman Key with a narrow incised band above and below the pattern. Both goblets have true square flat-bottomed bucket-shaped bowls, with medium height stems spread to a round foot. The color is dark mirror chrome silver, intact. Both retain their original cork seals in rough, sharp pontil scars. $1,600.00 pair

Blown non-lead glass footed beaker made in Bohemia circa 1860 – 1880, measuring 5¼" tall, with a deep cylindrical shaped bowl, short stem, and round foot. The piece is deep amber gold washed on the interior, and the outside is decorated with fine crystal granulate powder etching featuring a butterfly, a bird, ferns, leaves, and flora all around the piece. There are a series of etched narrow bands around the foot. The piece retains its original thin foil metal seal, slightly curled up and glass disc cemented into the rough pontil scar underfoot. The color is bright chrome, and the silvering is intact. $725.00

Blown flint glass footed goblet, made in the United States circa 1855 – 1870, probably Boston & Sandwich Glass Co. or the Boston Silver Glass Company, with a true flat bottomed bucket bowl, medium stem, and round foot. It retains its original cork seal in a rough pontil scar underfoot. The surface is plain mirror without embellishment, the color is dark bright chrome and the silvering is intact. $425.00

Blown flint glass footed goblet, made in the United States circa 1855 – 1870, probably Pennsylvania area, Dithridge & Co., measuring 6" tall with an unusually deep straight cylindrical bowl and a long stem spread to a round foot with a slight collar knop in the center of the stem. The piece is wheel engraved in a "vintage" pattern all around the outside surface of the bowl. The piece has a large cork seal in a rough pontil scar. The color is dark mirror chrome; the silvering intact. $550.00

Unusual blown lead glass footed beaker, made in Bohemia circa 1860 – 1880, measuring 5" tall, which is cased or stained in sapphire blue and wheel engraved in an intricate scenic pattern consisting of a deer, trees, and forest motifs in a center band which measures 1½" in width. There are three blue cased or stained bands around the top rim, collar knop, and top of the round foot, which are engraved with a series of ovals and dots. The piece retains its original seal consisting of a metal foil round and glass disc cemented into the smooth pontil scar underfoot. Unusual color and engraving. $850.00

Blown and molded non-lead glass footed beaker, made in Germany or Bohemia, measuring 5¼" tall, with a panel or rib pattern impressed on the inside of the piece, which is gold washed about half-way down the interior, and has granulate crystal etching consisting of leaves in various sizes and curling tendrils all around the piece. There is a narrow waisted stem and round foot, with two bands encircling the bottom of the stem and top of the round foot. The piece has its original metal seal and glass disc cemented loosely into the roughened pontil scar underfoot. $400.00

Blown and molded non-lead glass footed beaker, made in Bohemia circa 1860 –1880, measuring 5" tall, with a bright amber gold washed interior and ten wide molded panels giving a ribbed appearance, decorated with crushed crystal granulate etching in an unusual free-hand design featuring Rococo scrolls and curved swags all around the outside of the piece. The beaker has a short stem and round foot, and has a non-original cork covered by silver paper over the rough opened pontil hole underfoot. $450.00

Blown footed non-lead glass stemmed goblet, made in Bohemia or Germany circa 1860 – 1880, measuring 6¼" tall, with an acid-vapor satin matting surface on the serpentine rounded funnel bowl with a slightly inverted rim, and featuring cold painting and enamel in an intricate and unusual pattern of gold medallions, painted branches, berries, and leaves in spring green and turquoise accented by white enamel beading. There is a swag and drape effect to the design, and the stem has a collar knop spread to pedestal foot resting on a larger round bottom foot. The piece retains its original thin metal seal and glass disc cemented into the roughened pontil hole underfoot. There is some spottiness to the upper surface of the top rim and around the stem and foot. $600.00

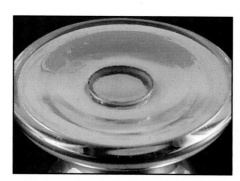

Blown non-flint glass goblet, made in Germany or Bohemia circa 1870 – 1890, measuring 4¾" tall, with a bright gold washed interior, and decorated with an unusual combination of oval cartouches, stylized flowers, and netting in the applied granulate etching technique. The piece has a flared top, and the diameter measures 3½" across the rim. The goblet retains its original metal seal and glass disc cemented into the polished pontil scar underfoot. $450.00

Blown flint glass footed goblet, made in the United States circa 1855 – 1870, featuring a delicate, wheel engraved "vintage" pattern, and measuring 5½" tall. The color is bright silver mirror, and the piece was probably made at the Boston & Sandwich Glass Company or the Boston Silver Glass Company. The goblet retains its original cork seal in the rough pontil scar, and has most of its red circular paper seal covering the cork seal. $450.00

Blown flint glass footed goblet, made in the United States circa 1855 – 1870, probably New England Glass Company, with a rare and unusual wheel-engraved pattern featuring intricate stylized "lace" festoons, ribbon bows, flowers, leaf chains, and swags all around the bucket-shaped bowl. The piece measures 6" tall, and has a deep, round foot. There is a cork and black wax substance in the rough pontil scar underfoot which does not appear to be original. There is some flaking loss to the outer foot rim. Rare engraved pattern. $650.00

Blown and molded non-flint glass footed goblet, made in Bohemia or Germany circa 1860 – 1880, with applied crushed crystal granule etching in a variant "vintage" pattern consisting of berries, leaves, vines, and curling tendrils. The goblet measures 5" tall and has a bright gold washed interior. The piece retains its original metal seal and glass disc cemented into the polished pontil scar underfoot. There is some cloudiness and spottiness to the upper surface of the foot, and the color is bright silver. $175.00

Blown and molded non-lead glass footed goblet, made in Bohemia circa 1850 – 1880, measuring 5½" tall, featuring a band of berries, leaves, and vines encircling the tapered cylindrical cup, with a medium length stem and round foot. The piece has a deep amber gold washed interior stained only halfway down the interior. The goblet has its original metal seal and glass disc inserted into the rough pontil scar underfoot. The glass has bubbles and striations and slight loss of silvering underfoot. $195.00

Blown and molded lead glass footed goblet, made in Germany or Bohemia circa 1860 – 1880, measuring 5½" tall and decorated with "ice" crystal granulate etching in a fine and detailed "vintage" pattern all around the outside of the deep cylindrical body. The interior is bright amber gold washed and the long stem has an unusual clear glass triple coin knop ending in a round foot. The silvering is bright metal. The piece retains its original metal seal and glass disc cemented into the smooth polished pontil scar underfoot. There is some minor clouding and loss of silver around the pontil scar underfoot. $250.00

Blown non-lead glass footed chalice with a round bowl, made in Bohemia or Germany circa 1860 – 1880, measuring 3¾" tall, decorated in dense granulate etching in a large-scale "vintage" pattern. The interior of the bowl is bright amber gold washed and the medium length stem has an oval knop. The piece retains its original metal seal and glass disc cemented into the smooth pontil scar underfoot. $300.00

Blown, non-flint glass diminutive sized footed goblet or cordial glass, made in Bohemia or Germany circa 1860 – 1880, measuring 3¼" tall, and decorated with an applied "vintage" pattern in the crystal granulate technique. The cordial has a bright medium amber gold washed interior bowl. It retains its original metal seal and glass disc cemented into the smooth pontil scar underfoot, which is large for the size of the piece. $125.00

Blown, lead glass footed goblet, made in Bohemia circa 1860 – 1880, measuring 5½" tall and decorated with the vintage pattern and a bird in the applied crystal granulate etch technique. The interior is bright amber gold washed. The piece retains its original lead seal and glass disc to the pontil opening underfoot. The silvering is intact with some minor haze to the top of the round foot. $195.00

Blown flint glass footed goblet, made in the United States circa 1855 – 1870, probably New England Glass Company, Cambridge, Massachusetts, measuring 5¼" tall, with a flared top bucket bowl, medium stem, and large, rounded foot. The goblet is decorated with fine wheel engraving consisting of a stylized leaf wreath, lower center bow, encircling the letters "S. A. M." in English script on one side, and the other side engraved in an expert engraved "vintage" pattern. The piece has its original thick glass plug inserted into the polished pontil scar underfoot. The color is bright mirror chrome silver. There is a line plate fracture underfoot with some clouded areas. $800.00

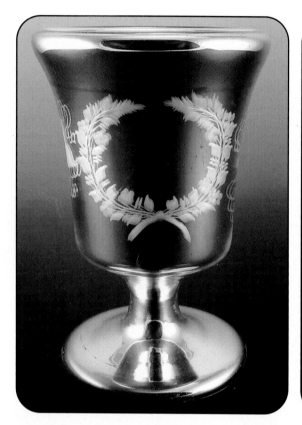

Blown flint glass footed goblet, made in the United States circa 1855 – 1870, probably New England Glass Company, Cambridge, Massachusetts, or possibly Boston & Sandwich Glass Company. The piece measures 6" tall with a bucket bowl, and has been wheel engraved with a stylized leaf wreath with a bow that is blank in the center. The back of the goblet is engraved in the "vintage" pattern. This piece may represent the theory that silvered glass items were initially engraved in advance, in preparation for further "custom" work, or merely, an unfinished specimen, though unlikely. The goblet is dark chrome mirror. It has its original cork seal imbedded in a rough pontil scar, and there is a large, circular silver paper seal that covers most of the bottom surface underfoot. $700.00

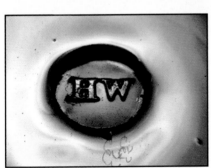

Matched pair of blown and molded lead glass presentation chalices, made in Bohemia circa 1860 – 1880, each measuring 9" tall, with a large round cup, collar knob, an pedestal stem spread to round foot, with rare jewel cabochons within and intricate combination of patterns consisting of large-scale grape leaves, curling tendrils and vines, fleur-de-lis chain and scroll banding, small-scale feathered leaf chain swags, and Byzantine medallions. There are bunches of stylized "grapes" consisting of 3 mm round, flat-back emerald tone cabochons, round, sapphire blue and ruby red pieces, and rich ruby teardrop jewels accenting the white, granulate etch work all around each chalice. The silvering is bright silver mirror chrome, with no loss of silvering, and the pair retain their original metal seal impressed "HW" for Hugo Wolf, with a glass disc inserted into the polished pontil scar underfoot. Some of the cabochons are missing. $5,000.00 pair

Blown non-lead glass handled mug, made in Bohemia or Germany circa 1860 – 1880, measuring 4½" tall with a bright amber gold washed interior and granulate-application powder etching with cold paint accents in an intricate grape leaf, vine, grapes, and tendrils pattern all around the outside surface. The handle is thick clear glass which was applied and finished with tine marks on the bottom. The piece retains its large metal plug and glass disc in a smooth polished pontil scar underfoot. The silvering is hazy and spotting in places with some minor patch loss underfoot. $225.00

Blown non-lead glass handled tankard, measuring 3½" tall, with a clear applied glass handle, made circa 1850 – 1880 in Germany or Bohemia, in a folk granulate-powder applied etching consisting of oversized grape leaves and tendrils. The piece has a gold stain on the interior and its original metal seal and glass disc cemented into the rough pontil scar underfoot. There is hazing and cloudiness on the interior surface of the piece, more noticeable at the bottom, and the glass has many small bubbles and minor striations consistent with soda-lime glass. $175.00

Blown non-lead glass footed child's mug, circa 1850 – 1870, probably Germany or Bohemia, with a bright amber stained interior and rustic hand-applied granulate-powder etching "For a Good Boy," probably made for export to England or the United States. The piece measures 3¼" tall with an applied clear glass handle, with a non-original cork in the rough pontil scar underfoot. $125.00

Blown non-flint glass handled mug, measuring 4" tall, circa 1850 – 1880, made in Bohemia or Germany with a bright gold washed interior and applied crystal granulate etched pattern consisting of a bird, berries, leaves, vines, and curling tendrils all around the curved corset shaped cup, finished with a clear applied glass handle. The glass has bubbles and striations throughout. The piece retains its original metal plug and glass disc cemented into the rough pontil scar underfoot. $200.00

Blown non-lead glass footed mug, made in Bohemia circa 1855 – 1880, measuring 4" tall with a deep amber gold washed interior and applied, clear glass handle. The piece is decorated with applied granulate powder etching in a "vintage" pattern. The piece has a platform foot, and retains its original foil closure and glass disc underfoot cemented into the polished pontil scar. $195.00

Blown non-flint glass handled tankard, made in Bohemia circa 1855 – 1880, measuring 3¾" tall, and featuring unusual white enamel hand-painted leaves, grapes, and tendrils all around the outside surface. The handle is clear glass and applied. The piece has a glass disc glued to the pontil scar underfoot, which is not original to the piece. There is clouding and spottiness of the silvering underfoot. $150.00

Blown footed tankard, measuring 4¾" tall, with a clear, thick, applied glass handle, straight sided cylindrical bowl, narrow stem, and round foot. The piece is light bright silver color and decorated with superficial etching in a grape leaf and tendril pattern. The piece has its original metal seal and glass disc cemented into a rough pontil scar underfoot. $195.00

Silvered mercury glass compotes and chalices were made in Bohemia, England, Germany, and the United States. The compote form, which is a bowl on stem or foot, was originally created to hold fruit, and the word "compote" refers to mixed fruit. Compotes in silvered mercury glass, as with vases and goblet forms, were subject to many of the same decorative treatments including hand painting, enameling, and etching, though most commonly, the granulate crystal application process. In fact, most compotes in this chapter, which were made in Bohemia, have some form of granulate etching in white on a silvery ground with a typical interior treatment of bright amber gold wash. The bowl of the compote, with its wide, open diameter, is so obvious upon visual inspection that the combination of silver and gold is truly most dramatic in this form. The aesthetic balance of bowl and stem, together with decorations of the finest artistic merit, make the compote a choice centerpiece for the table, and although utilitarian in shape and form, these luxury pieces were likely made just for "show."

Most compotes were made in Bohemia, as evidenced by the more lightweight non-flint glass composition as well as both the decorating and sealing techniques. In the United States, compotes were made of flint glass, and often much larger in dimension and height when compared to the Bohemian examples. Compotes were also made in England, and subject to the cut through layering comparable to the vase forms, although no specimen is was available for photographic presentation in this chapter. Plain, silvered chalice forms made by Varnish and Thomson are illustrated in this book. As compared to the Bohemian examples, compotes made in England and the United States are much heavier in weight.

The chalice form, which strictly describes the bowl on foot used in the presentation of the Eucharist, has a slightly different proportion and dimension. Where the typical compote has a gradient slope beginning at the rim, the chalice form usually has a wide pan rim and a deep and narrow bottom dimension. While no authentication is possible, it is likely that some silvered mercury glass chalices could have been used during the Christian liturgy.

Most compotes were made strictly as open pieces, although a rare covered example is included in this chapter. Although actual dimensions vary, most compotes range from about five to six inches tall, and have a top bowl diameter of five to seven inches. When compared to vases and goblet forms, compotes and chalices were simply not produced in the same quantity and therefore, surviving examples in good condition are considered rare.

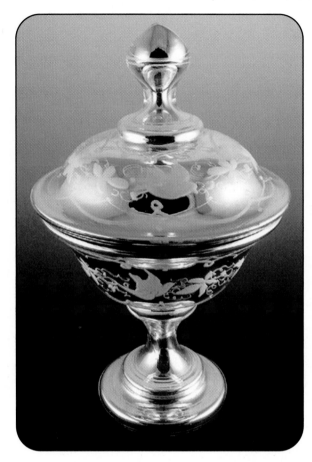

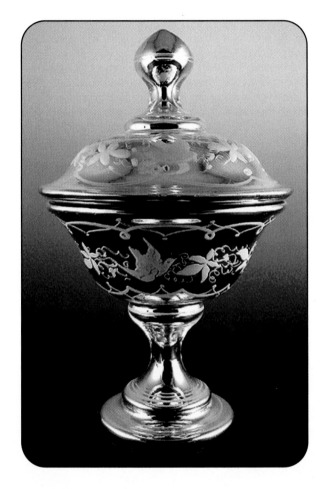

Covered Bohemian blown and molded glass compote, made circa 1860 – 1880, measuring 10½" tall with cover, and decorated with applied crushed crystal granulate etching, in an all-over pattern consisting of birds and the grape vine and leaf "vintage" design, together with thin interposed arched banding that frames the design, and other concentric fine banding on the stem, and on the top surface of the cover, as well as the finial handle. The interior bowl of the compote is a deep copper gold wash, and both the compote and cover retain their original metal foil seal covered with a glass disc cemented into a polished pontil scar underfoot and under the cover. The deep bowl measures 6½" in diameter, and the stem has a collar knop at the top, and ends in a pedestal atop the rounded foot. The silvering is intact and mirror bright without loss. $3,000.00

Blown non-flint glass, made in Bohemia circa 1860 – 1880, measuring 5¼" tall, with a bright gold washed interior and decorating with applied granulate etching in a dense pattern with birds, reeds, vines, and leaves, and narrow banding around the stem knop and top surface of the rounded foot. The bowl measures 5½" in diameter, and the stem has a large, flat oval knop measuring almost 2" across. The piece has its original metal seal and glass disc cemented into a smoothed pontil scar underfoot. The silvering is all intact and bright. $950.00

Blown and molded Bohemian lead crystal glass footed compote, made in Bohemia or Germany circa 1860 – 1880, featuring an unusual Gothic pattern consisting of arches, geometric cross-banding, intricate leaf chain and filigree lattice work with a coarse crushed granulate etching resembling ice crystals. The surface of the granulate etch work is gritty to the touch, and the pattern sparkles in the light. The compote measures 6" tall and the diameter of the deep bowl measures 5¾" across. The spread platform bottom shaped bowl has a deep bright gold washed interior, and the long stem has a slight center round knop, spread to a molded pedestal atop the rounded foot. The silvering is bright mirror chrome and all intact. The piece retains its original metal seal and glass disc snugly fitted into the polished pontil scar underfoot. The glass is highly resonant with a deep bell tone, and the piece is heavy for its size, with an unusual and rare artistic quality. $1,250.00

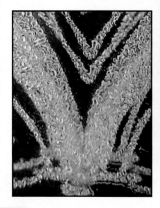

Blown and molded non-lead glass open compote, made in Bohemia circa 1860 – 1880, with a light gold washed interior, and measuring 6½" tall with a wide and deep bowl measuring 7½" in diameter. The stem has a large, flattened ovoid knop then spreads to foot. Decorated with applied granulate etching featuring large, stylized palmetto leaves, ferns, and grass, with gradient etched bands encircling the bottom of the exterior bowl, stem knop, and lower top surface of the rounded foot. The silvering is intact with minor light spotting to the outside foot rim. The piece retains its original lead seal cemented into rough pontil scar underfoot. $850.00

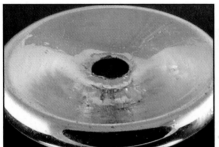

Blown and molded non-flint glass footed compote, made in Bohemia or Germany circa 1860 – 1880, with an acid-vapor satin-mat ground, and decorated with applied cold enameling in a geometric based pattern, consisting of scrolls and other continuous banding which is painted in gold. There is additional sheer blue painted rings above and below the wide gold banding and thin blue lines outlining the frosted satin surfaces on the stem and foot. The interior bowl is plain bright mirror silver. The piece retains its original lead seal and glass disc cemented into the rough pontil scar underfoot. The stem has an irregular indentation flaw, probably caused by improper handling during the annealing phase and done during manufacturing. There is some surface wear to the raised enameled surfaces. $875.00

Blown, molded non-lead glass compote, made in Bohemia or Germany circa 1860 – 1880, with a shallow, wide cup-shaped and light copper gold washed bowl, and decorated with dense and intricate vintage patterning, consisting of leaves, grapes, grape leaves, and curling tendrils and vines, in the applied crystal granulate technique all around the outside surface of the bowl. With an unusual bell-shaped pedestal stem spreading to a round bottom foot, the piece measures 5½" tall with a 5¼" top rim diameter. There are a series of concentric narrow rings banding to the lower third of the pedestal stem and a chain of vintage vine patterning around the outside top foot rim surface. The piece retains its original metal seal and glass disc cemented into the rough pontil scar

underfoot. The silvering is all intact and the surfaces are bright light mirror chrome. $775.00

Blown and molded non-flint glass footed chalice, made in Bohemia or Germany circa 1870 – 1890, featuring a light, bright gold washed interior, round funnel-shaped deep bowl, which measures 5¼" in diameter and 5½" tall. The exterior bowl surface is decorated with a large stylized leaf, vine, and berry pattern with two birds perched on branches in the applied granulate crystal etch technique. The stem is a baluster shape ending in a short platform atop a round spread foot. The piece has its original lead seal and glass disc cemented into the rough pontil scar underfoot. The silvering is intact and bright mirror chrome with no loss. $750.00

Blown and molded non-lead Bohemian crystal glass footed compote, made circa 1860 – 1880, with a round cup-shaped bowl that is gold washed and decorated on the exterior surface with birds, grape clusters, grape leaves, and vines in the granulate etch technique. The stem is unusually long with a double round knop, spreading into a large round foot decorated with narrow concentric and arched banding. The piece measures 6¼" tall with a deep bowl measuring 5¾" in diameter. The silvering is dark chrome mirror and all intact. The piece retains its original lead seal and glass disc cemented into the slightly polished pontil scar underfoot. $825.00

Blown, molded non-flint glass footed compote, made in Bohemia circa 1860 – 1880, with a gold washed interior, wide, shallow bowl that measures 5½" in diameter and 5¾" tall. The outside surfaces are decorated with the dense granulate applied etching in an allover "vintage" pattern consisting of large stylized grape leaves, vines, and curling tendrils on the exterior surface of the bowl and around the outer area of the top foot. There is a large collar pedestal under the bowl with a flattened, oval knop on the tall stem, which is spread to the round and deep foot. The piece has its original light metal seal and glass disc cemented into the rough pontil scar underfoot. There is some minor spottiness on the upper edge and under the foot. $525.00

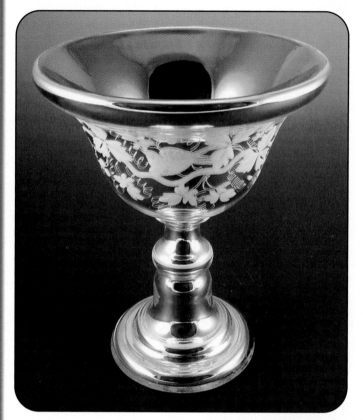

Blown and molded footed chalice of non-lead Bohemian crystal, circa 1860 – 1880, featuring a deep amber gold washed bowl in a round and deep funnel shape with a slight top rim pan, and decorated with dense and intricate pattern with the applied crystal granulate technique, consisting of grapes, grape leaves, vines, curling tendrils, and branches with two birds perched among the foliage. The chalice is 6¼" tall and the open top diameter measures 5½" across the rim. The stem has a short narrow top with an oval knop on top of a bell-shaped pedestal atop the round bottom foot. The surfaces are

bright mirror chrome. The piece retains its original large metal seal and glass disc cemented into the slightly smoothed pontil scar underfoot. $975.00

Blown and molded footed compote, made circa 1860 – 1880 in Bohemia or Germany, of Bohemian crystal glass, with a large, round cup-shaped bowl resting atop a wide round pillar-shaped pedestal base spread to bottom foot, and decorated with an intricate larger scale vintage pattern. The interior of the bowl is bright gold washed. The piece measures 6¼" tall and an open top diameter of 5¾" across the rim. The lower portion of the pedestal stem is slightly yellowed with some interior clouding of the silvering underfoot. The piece retains its original foil seal and glass disc, which are large for their size, cemented into the rough pontil scar underfoot. $625.00

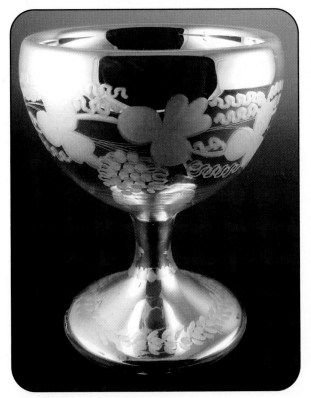

Blown flint glass footed chalice made circa 1855 – 1870 possibly by the Boston & Sandwich Glass Company, Boston Silver Glass Company, or the Union Glass Company, New England area, United States, featuring surface copper-wheel engraved designs consisting of grape clusters, large, stylized grape leaves, and curling tendrils around the exterior surface of the deep, cup-shaped bowl. There are additional engraved areas around the outer edge of the foot rim, consisting of a leaf chain and a series of circle dots around the lower stem. The piece measures 6" tall, and the bowl measures 4½" across the rim. The chalice is very heavy for its size. It has a cork seal inserted into the rough pontil scar underfoot. There are remnants of a rectangular shaped paper label consistent with

the style used in the third quarter nineteenth century. The silvering is deep dark mirror chrome, with several small areas of flaking on the outside foot rim. $575.00

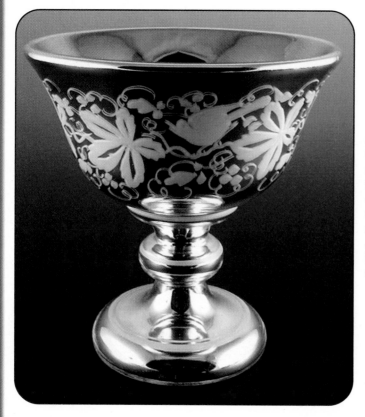

Blown and molded non-flint glass footed chalice, made in Bohemia or Germany circa 1860 – 1880, with a bird and "vintage" pattern and narrow banding, done with the applied crystal granulate etch technique around the exterior surface of the deep amber gold washed bowl. The bowl is deep and has a round funnel shape, and the stem is short and thick with a mid-range oval knop spread to the round foot. The piece measures 5¼" tall and the top diameter is 5¼" across the rim. The piece is bright mirror silver. Its original metal seal and glass disc cemented into the polished pontil hole underfoot. $650.00

Blown and molded non-lead Bohemian crystal glass footed compote, made circa 1860 – 1880, measuring 4¾" tall, and featuring a well-executed "vintage" pattern with intricate detail and defined grape leaves, bunches of grapes, curling tendrils, and branches arched around the exterior surface of the light copper gold washed bowl. The piece has a plain and straight stem, spread to a round foot, which is further decorated with a small scale "vintage" pattern chain in the same granulate crystal etch technique. The bowl is deep and wide and measures 5½" across the top. The piece retains its original metal seal and glass disc, which are large for size, cemented into the polished pontil scar underfoot. $600.00

Blown lead glass footed chalice, made in England circa 1849 – 1855, measuring 7" tall with a deep, bell-shaped bowl, flared pan rim and baluster stem. The glass is highly resonant and extremely heavy for its size, in a bright mirror chrome color. The open diameter measures 6" across the rim. The compote retains its original impressed metal disc and glass seal, fitted into the polished pontil holes underfoot. The seal is impressed with the words Varnish & Co., Patent London. The rim measures 4½" in diameter and shows wear marks normal for age. $5,500.00

Blown flint glass footed chalice, made in the United States, possibly Dithridge & Company, Pennsylvania or New England, circa 1855 – 1870, measuring 8¼" tall with a deep, round bowl measuring 8¼" across the rim. The bowl and pedestal stem have been blown separately, and the stem, with a reverse baluster shape spread to foot, has its original cork seal inserted into the rough pontil scar underfoot. The bowl is wheel engraved with the initials "ML" in old English script, and has been attached to the pedestal stem. The piece is extremely heavy for its size, and highly resonant with a deep bell tone when tapped. Color is deep mirror chrome with all silvering intact. $1,500.00

Blown molded non-flint glass tall footed compote, made in Bohemia circa 1860 – 1880, measuring 7" tall, and decorated with the applied crushed crystal granulate etching technique in an intricate design consisting of birds, stylized leaves, vines, berries, and curling tendrils with a stylized geometric leaf vine band around the top and bottom of the panel all around the exterior of the bright amber gold washed bowl. The bowl rests on a collar base, with a long stem ending in a platform pedestal atop a rounded platform foot. The bowl measures 6½" across the top diameter from rim to rim, and the color is bright silver mirror with all silvering intact. The piece retains its original lead seal and glass disc cemented into the rough pontil scar underfoot. $1,150.00

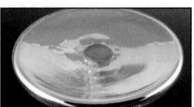

Blown and molded non-lead glass compote on pedestal base, made in Bohemia circa 1870 – 1890, and decorated with the applied granulate etching technique in a combination of patterns. The bowl is deep amber gold washed, and the exterior pattern consists of palm trees, ferns, and leaves all around the piece. The pedestal base is decorated in complimentary pattern consisting of various stylized leaves and branches, as well as a series of bands in varying widths. The piece measures 7½" tall, and open top bowl diameter measures 5½" from rim to rim. There is some cloudiness and silvering loss to the lower third of the pedestal. The piece retains its original metal seal and glass disc cemented in the rough pontil scar underfoot. $750.00

Blown, molded non-flint glass, made in Bohemia or Germany circa 1860 – 1880, this footed compote measures 6½" tall with an open top diameter of 6¼" across the rim. The shallow, wide flaring bowl is decorated with a large scale "vintage" pattern consisting of stylized grape leaves, vines, branches, and curling tendrils around the exterior surface in the granulate crystal etching technique. There is a series of granulate applied concentric bands around the top surface of the foot and around the knop and stem. The stem has a molded acorn-shaped knop, and the lower stem spreads to a round foot. The silvering is light bright mirror silver. The piece retains its original lead seal and glass disc cemented into the rough pontil scar underfoot. $950.00

Blown, molded non-lead glass footed compote, made in Bohemia circa 1860 – 1880, with a large, flared deep gold washed bowl resting on a collar base, curving into an oval knop, and a short stem that spreads to a deep, and large rounded foot. The compote measures 6¾" tall with a 7¼" wide open diameter. The exterior surface is decorated in a well-executed "vintage" pattern with fine, curly tendrils, small and large grape leaves, and birds on branches around the bowl. There is a wide ½" band of granulate etching on the top surface of the deep rounded foot. The piece retains its original lead seal and glass disc which is slightly pushed into the rough pontil scar underfoot. The silvering is light mirror color with some minor hazing underfoot. $875.00

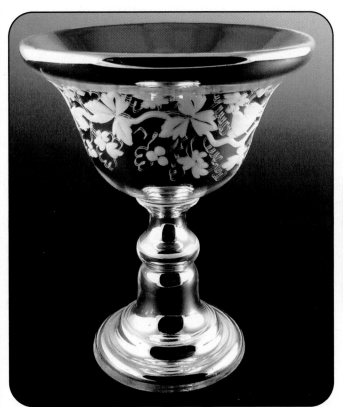

Blown and molded non-flint glass footed compote, made in Bohemia circa 1860 – 1880, with a deep, medium amber gold washed bowl, measuring 6¼" tall with a wide, 6¾" open top diameter. The piece is decorated with the applied crystal granulate etching in a pattern consisting of birds, leaves, vines, and curling tendrils all around the exterior of the bowl. There are a series of varying sized narrow bands around the stem, knop, and foot, with the lower stem ending in a slightly raised molded pedestal atop the large foot. There is some haziness, spotting, and patch loss to the

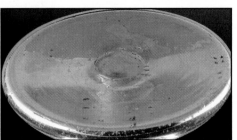

silvering under-foot. The piece retains its original metal seal and glass disc cemented into a rough pontil scar under-foot. $750.00

Blown and molded non-flint glass compote, made in Bohemia or Germany circa 1860 – 1880, measures 4½" tall and 5½" across the open bowl rim. The bowl is a deep amber gold wash, and the exterior surface is decorated in the "vintage" pattern, alternating with birds in flight, with the applied dense granulate application technique. The piece has its original metal seal cemented into the rough pontil scar underfoot. There are bubbles and striations in the glass, and some small areas of cloudiness on the upper surface of the bowl. $425.00

Blown flint glass tall footed compote, made in the United States circa 1855 – 1870, probably in New England at the Boston & Sandwich Glass Company, measuring 7½" tall with a large, wide, and deep bowl measuring 7" in diameter across the rim. The bowl is decorated with a copper wheel engraved design consisting of lady ferns and stylized royal ferns, with particular artistic merit and graceful detail. The long stem is a true baluster shape, which was hand marvered, and ends in a large, round foot. The color is bright mirror chrome, and the compote is extremely heavy for its size. The piece retains its original cork seal embedded into the rough pontil scar, with remnants of a silver colored circular paper label. $1,800.00

Blown flint glass footed compote, measuring 7½" tall, made in the United States, probably Boston Silver Glass Company or Union Glass Company, circa 1855 – 1870. The stem is medium width with a slight balustroid shape at the bottom, which curves in then spreads to a large, rounded foot. The color is bright mirror chrome. The piece retains its original cork seal fitted into the rough pontil scar, with tiny remnants of a silver colored paper seal. The compote is extremely heavy for its size, and the glass has a high bell tone resonance when tapped. $1,200.00

Blown flint glass footed compote, made in the United States, possibly Boston & Sandwich Glass or another New England maker, circa 1855 – 1870. The compote measures 6¼" tall with a wide sloping deep bowl measuring 7" across the rim. The stem is slightly curved and spread to a large, round foot. The color is bright mirror chrome. The piece retains its original cork in the rough pontil scar underfoot. $1,000.00

Very large presentation footed compote, made of blown flint glass, circa 1855 – 1870, possibly Boston Silver Glass Company or Union Glass Company, and measuring 7½" tall with a large, deep bowl measuring 8½" across the rim. The stem is medium width and length, with a slight mock baluster bottom bulge, then spread to a deep and well turned foot with unusual height. The piece has a large cork and wax in the rough pontil scar as found. Some cloudiness and patch loss on one side of the foot, and extremely heavy for its size. The color is deep mirror chrome. $1,000.00

Blown, lead glass chalice, made in England circa 1849 – 1855, and measuring 7¼" tall, with cased gold glass interior bowl with a flared pan rim that measures 6" in diameter. The stem has a collar top and deep curve, then flares to a baluster shape at the bottom, atop a large, rounded foot that measures 4½" across. The color is brilliant silver mirror. The piece retains its original metal seal, impressed Varnish & Co., Patent London under a glass disc which is fitted into the polished pontil scar underfoot. Silvering is all intact, and the piece is extremely heavy for its size. $6,000.00

Blown flint glass footed chalice, made in England circa 1855 – 1860, measuring 6¾" tall, with a deep flared pan rimmed bowl measuring 6" in diameter. The stem has a round collar top and deep baluster bottom spread to a large, rounded foot measuring 4¼" wide. The piece has its original metal seal impressed Thomson's Patent London covered with a round glass disc fitted into the polished pontil scar underfoot. The silvering is bright mirror color, and piece is extremely heavy for its size. $5,500.00

Blown flint glass footed compote, made in the United States circa 1855 – 1870, probably Boston & Sandwich Glass Company or Boston Silver Glass Company, measuring 6½" tall with a deep, large round bowl measuring 8" in diameter. The outside surface is wheel engraved in the "vintage" pattern, which features open grape clusters, curling tendrils, stylized leaves, and flowers. The piece has a slightly knopped stem spread to a large, round foot and is very heavy for its size. Has its original seal, unknown material in the rough pontil scar underfoot that is covered with a silver and red paper seal. $1,200.00

Blown and marvered lead glass footed compote, made in Bohemia or Germany circa 1860 – 1880, measuring 4½" tall with a deep, bucket shaped bowl, medium stem in baluster form, and decorated with quartz crystal granulate etching in an intricate "vintage" pattern consisting of grapes, leaves, vines, and curling tendrils and concentric banding to the stem and foot. The interior of the bowl is bright amber gold washed. The compote retains its original lead seal and glass disc cemented into the smooth pontil scar underfoot. The pontil round opening is large for the size of the compote. The color is bright chrome and the silvering is intact. $325.00

Blown and molded non-lead glass footed compote, made in Germany or Bohemia circa 1860 – 1880, measuring 5" tall with an open top diameter of 5" and decorated in a dense granulate application etch technique in a pattern consisting of vines, grape leaves, and curling tendrils. The interior of the bowl is bright gold wash. The compote retains its original lead seal without a glass disc inserted into the rough pontil scar underfoot. There are bubbles, striations and some speckling to the silver. $450.00

Blown and molded lead glass footed presentation compote, made in Germany or Bohemia, measuring 6" tall and 6" across the open bowl diameter. The compote is wheel engraved in German "Dem Silberbrautpaar. Den 11th Jan 1873," which translates into "silver brides," likely made as a commemorative piece to mark the wedding day or 25th anniversary of a married couple. Unusual to find combination of engraved and etched motifs, consisting of birds, vines, leaves, and curling tendrils all around the top surface of the pan-shaped bowl. The interior is

bright amber gold washed. The piece retains its original lead seal and glass disc underfoot cemented into the round pontil scar. There is cloudiness and some silvering loss to the foot and interior bowl. $950.00

Tableware: Creamers, Pitchers, Sugar Bowls, and Salts

In silvered mercury glass, as with many other forms of glassware, a variety of service forms were made in utilitarian shapes. Less common than goblets and compotes, creamers, pitchers, sugar bowls, waste bowls, and saltcellars were made with blown flint glass as well as the non-flint, lightweight soda lime glass of Continental origin. Additional specialty items, such as smoking sets and unusual receptacles were made even less frequently, and examples are rare to find.

Pitchers and pouring creamers were usually blown in one piece, and clear glass handles were applied as a separate step as shown on page 25. American-made cream pitchers, such as the style patented by John Haines in 1874, have applied metal spouts, often bearing the patent date. Table sets, often decorated with either engraved or etched designs, were made in the United States and Bohemia, although rare to find. Surviving examples sometimes have custom engraved dates, and were probably made as commemorative pieces. Creamers, covered sugar bowls, open waste bowls, spooners, and goblets were made as sets, and the accompanying goblets are featured in this chapter, rather than in Beakers, Goblets, Mugs, and Pokals. Sugar bowl covers were made of thin molded flint glass which was wheel engraved in a pattern to match the bowl, or, in other pieces, made of double-walled glass that was silvered. In these cases, the sugar bowl is extremely heavy, and it is likely that silvered mercury tableware was used more for ornament than service. In either case, an additional marveling or molding step was necessary to fabricate the rim insert, in order for the cover to conform to the bottom piece.

Generally, Bohemian or German tableware seemed to have been made less frequently, as examples are hard to find. When comparing Bohemian and German ware to the United States, utilitarian table pieces are much less common. Luxury glass, by Continental standards, seemed more relegated to the vase, chalice, or goblet form, whereas, glass made in the United States, including silvered mercury glass, appears in forms that are useful, as well as decorative. From the mid-nineteenth century and continuing until at least the last decade, most American glass was made in utilitarian form. American silvered mercury glass can be found with custom engraving, as evidenced by examples from the illustrations to follow.

In addition to creamers, pitchers, sugars, and accompanying goblet forms, both master salt holders and individual salt holders or saltcellars were made in silvered mercury glass. Saltcellars tend to be of either American or English origin, though occasional Bohemian examples can be found. Regardless of the glass form, saltcellars seem to be more common in England and the United States, as compared to Continental Europe.

Important three-piece blown flint silvered mercury American glass presentation set, wheel engraved and dated Dec. 14th 1864, consisting of a cream pitcher, goblet, and covered sugar bowl. The creamer measures 7" tall including an applied metal spout. The piece has a thick, clear glass handle in the so called "ear" shape, which was tine pressed to the surface of the body while semi-molten. What is most notable, is the fact that although the engraved date year is clearly 1864, the patent granted to John Haines concerning the improvement for silvering glass pitchers, which depicts the applied metal top in the patent illustration, was not granted until April 4, 1865. This could indicate that the use and application of metal spouts for silvered glass pitchers were not inherently the only technical enhancement for "improving" silvered glass pitchers. The fact that this pitcher exists provides a clue that a metal spout was used before the John Haines patent was actually granted.

The covered sugar bowl, measuring 7½" tall, has a clear glass top with a round, raised finial handle that was blown in one piece. The tip of the finial has been ground to smooth the blowpipe scar, so the handle has a flat top. The matching footed goblet measures 5¾" tall and all three pieces have an additional wreath comprised of stylized leaves and a bow, outlining the engraved dates on the piece, in addition to the "vintage" pattern on the back of all three items. The pieces retain their original cork inserted into the small rough pontil scar underfoot. The silvering is all intact and bright mirror chrome. This set could have been made by the Boston Silver Glass Company, which was organized in 1857, or the Boston and Sandwich Glass Company. $7,000.00

Blown flint glass footed pitcher, made in America circa 1855 – 1870, likely Boston Silver Glass Company or the Boston & Sandwich Glass Company, measuring 6⅞" tall, with a metal spout, according to John Haines patent, with an applied clear glass handle, and wheel engraved in a rustic stylized "vintage" pattern consisting of grapes, grape leaves, curling tendrils, and vines all around the tapered bulbous body. The pitcher retains its original cork in the large, unpolished pontil scar underfoot. The color is deep chrome silver and the piece is very heavy for its size. $1,400.00

Blown, flint glass footed cream pitcher, made in America probably at the Boston Silver Glass Company, and measuring 6½" tall. The metal spout is impressed: Patented April 4, 1865, according the John Haines patent. The pitcher has a thick clear glass applied handle with tine impressions and rollout along the bottom where the handle base meets the body. The piece retains its original cork, small for its size, in the rough pontil hole underfoot. There are small areas of cloudiness to the top of the foot rim and another small area on the surface of the exterior body. The color is dark mirror chrome. $1,250.00

Large blown flint glass pitcher, with a formed spout and applied clear glass handle, made in the United States circa 1855 – 1870, measuring 6½" tall, and decorated with wheel engraved grapes, grape leaves, vines, and curling tendrils. Likely made at the Boston & Sandwich Glass Company or possibly the New England Glass Company. The piece retains its original cork seal in the rough pontil scar underfoot. $950.00

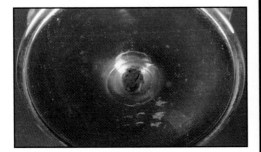

Blown flint glass footed waste bowl or possibly open sugar bowl, made in America circa 1855 – 1870, measuring 5¼" tall with a round, cup-shaped bowl, and wheel engraved in the "vintage" pattern all around the body. The piece was likely made in the Boston area, possibly the Boston & Sandwich Glass Company, and retains its original cork in the rough pontil scar, partially covered with a circular reddish foil paper seal underfoot. The color is bright chrome silver. $750.00

Blown flint glass taper holder or presentation piece, made in American circa 1855 – 1870, probably Boston & Sandwich Glass Company or other New England maker, measuring 6½" tall with an unusual floriform waisted tulip-shaped bowl, and richly wheel engraved with the initials "R. M. H." in old English script. This unusual shape, likely created by a combination of shaping, marvering, and compressing while the glass was semi-molten, was achieved without a mold, as the mid-bowl "bulge" does not have a concurrent indentation on the inner wall surface. There is tactile evidence of slight striation rings, similar to the surface lines evident in true wheel-thrown pottery, which would be consistent with slight pulling and shaping on the marver table, worked by the glassblower. There is a semi-wreath with a stylized bow encircling the script initials. The color is bright chrome silver and there is some minor cloudiness and thinning of the silvering on the top portion of the foot. The piece retains its original cork seal in the unpolished pontil scar. $1,100.00

Blown flint glass cigar holder, made in American circa 1860 – 1880, Dithridge & Co. or other Pennsylvania maker, measuring 6" tall with a square shaped cylindrical bowl, and wheel engraved with the word "SEGARS" within a scroll wreath consisting of leaves, together with grapes, grape vines, leaves, and curling tendrils around the back of the piece. There is a medium length stem with a slight bulge knop, then spread to a large, round foot. The color is deep chrome silver. The piece retains its original cork seal in the rough pontil scar underfoot. $1,000.00

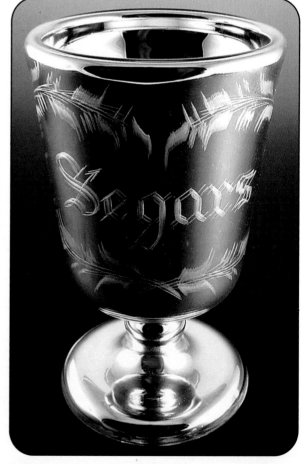

Blown presentation footed bowl, made in the United States circa 1855 – 1870, probably New England Glass Co., Boston & Sandwich, or other New England area company, measuring 5" in height, with a round, cup-shaped bowl with a 14" circumference, and wheel engraved with the initials "M.C.S. to T.G." enclosed in a leaf and floral wreath with a stylized bow. According to the seller, who was described as a direct descendant, the piece was a custom-made presentation piece received from a suitor. The color is bright chrome silver. The piece retains its original cork seal in the unpolished pontil scar underfoot, with remnants of a reddish and foil paper label. $1,400.00

Blown flint glass taper holder, made in the United States circa 1855 – 1870, measuring 6½" tall, with an unusual form bowl, similar to the RMH piece on page 122, and is wheel engraved in a large scale "vintage" pattern consisting of grapes, grape leaves, vines, and curling tendrils. The piece retains its original cork seal to the rough pontil scar underfoot, with part of a reddish foil paper seal consistent with Boston & Sandwich Glass pieces. The color is bright chrome silver and the silvering is intact. $950.00

Blown flint glass spooner, made in the United States circa 1855 – 1870, measuring 5" tall with a squat, bucket-shaped bowl, large foot, and engraved in a dense and intricate "vintage" pattern consisting of well-defined grape leaves, grape clusters, vines, and curling tendrils from the rim to the bottom of the bowl. The piece retains its original cork seal inserted into the rough pontil scar underfoot. The color is bright mirror silver, and the piece is very heavy for its size. $750.00

Blown molded cobalt and silvered mercury glass console bowl, attributed to the Mount Washington or Pairpoint Glass Works, New Bedford, Massachusetts, and made circa 1875 – 1890. The bowl is a round, cup shape, and the piece measures 5½" tall, with an open top diameter of 7¼". The pedestal base, made of blown and molded double-walled silvered mercury glass, measures 5¼" in diameter. Both pieces appear to have been joined together with a cement-like material, and the base has a cork in the pontil scar, with ordinary melted wax over it, and not original to the piece. $750.00

Unusual blown and molded cobalt and silvered flint glass console bowl. Possibly made in the United States at Mount Washington or Pairpoint Manufacturing Company, both of New Bedford, Massachusetts, circa 1875 – 1890. Both companies, which eventually merged in 1894, produced many types of art glass. Although speculative, the combination glass may have been made to counter the imported Bohemian glass items, which began to flood the American market in the closing decades of the nineteenth century. The piece measures 5⅞" tall overall including the pedestal base. The cobalt blue glass bowl has a deep, narrow bottom with a wide, flaring rim that measures 8¾" across the open diameter. The pedestal base, made separately of blown and molded double-walled silvered glass, measures 5½" across the bottom, and has a cork in the rough pontil scar. Both the cobalt bowl and silvered glass base were joined together with a cement-like material that can be seen close-up. Since Bohemian and Continental silvered mercury glass, in general, used metal seals and glass discs, the cork seal could well be a clue to its American origin. $800.00

Blown and molded non-flint glass footed tazza, made in Bohemia or Germany circa 1860 – 1880, and decorated with a combination of patterns in the applied granulate etching technique. The center of the tazza has a stylized floriform emblem, surrounded by a scroll and arch double ring. There is a band of grapevines, grape leaves, and curling tendrils, and a final scroll and arch double ring around the rim. There are a series of bands in various widths around the bell-shaped stem and pedestal foot. The piece retains its original metal seal with glass disc cemented into the smoothed pontil scar underfoot. $1,150.00

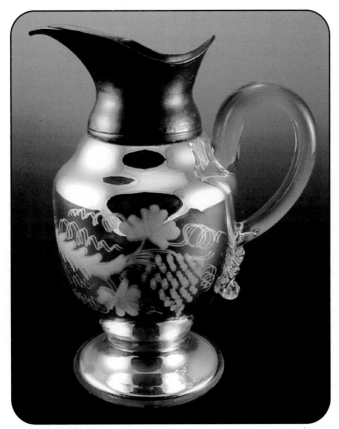

Blown flint glass cream pitcher with applied metal spout resembling Britannia, made in the United States circa 1860 – 1880, according to John Haines patent, but not marked, with an unusual sloped barrel shape, applied clear glass handle with crimped and turned finish, and measuring 6½" tall from the tip of the spout. Made by the Boston Silver Glass Company or the Boston & Sandwich Glass Company. The piece is wheel engraved in the "vintage" pattern, consisting of a combination of elongated stylized leaves, grape leaves, grape clusters, and curling tendrils all around the body, which tapers slightly and spreads to a short round foot. The pitcher retains its original cork seal in the rough pontil scar, and is unusually heavy for its size. The color is bright mirror chrome silver, and the handle has minor roughness along the lower portion of the handle adjacent to the crimping. $1,250.00

Blown flint glass cream pitcher with an unmarked applied silver-plated spout, measuring 6¾" tall, made in the United States circa 1860 – 1880 by the Boston Silver Glass Company or the Boston & Sandwich Glass Company, with a rounded then tapered body, applied clear glass handle finished with the typical crimped and turned method, with a narrow foot, and medium round spread foot. The piece is wheel engraved in an undulating "vintage" pattern consisting of grape clusters, well-veined grape leaves, and intricate curling tendrils. The color is bright mirror chrome silver. The piece retains its original cork seal in the small pontil scar underfoot, showing remnants of a circular reddish color paper seal. There is one small pencil eraser sized cloudy spot on the outside rim of the foot. $1,400.00

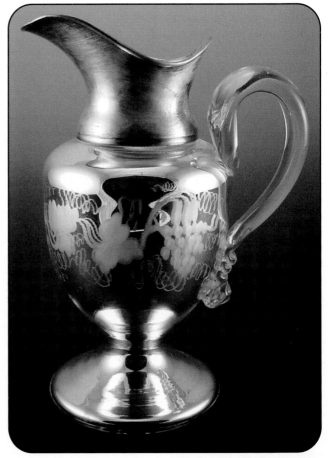

Blown flint glass footed sugar bowl with cover, made in the United States circa 1855 – 1880, with a round, cup-shape narrow stem and medium spread foot, and decorated with a wheel engraved pattern consisting of flowers, grape leaves, grape clusters, vines, and tendrils. The matching top, made of clear glass, and engraved in a matching pattern, has an applied ball finial handle, as opposed to other examples, which were blown in one piece. The covered sugar bowl measures 8" tall with the top. It has a cork seal inserted into the rough pontil scar, which may not be original to the piece. The color is bright mirror chrome silver, and there is some minor patch loss of the silvering around the foot rim. $850.00

Blown flint glass bowl, with a blown, silvered top, made in the United States circa 1860 – 1880, possibly by the New England Glass Company, and measuring 8½" tall with its cover. The bowl has a square, bucket shape and is unusually deep and large, and may have been used as a table vessel to keep sugar or another substance. The footed bowl is decorated with a fine wheel engraved pattern consisting of ferns, well-defined and detailed birch tree style leaves, and botanically correct flowers amidst a serpentine leaf vine which encircles the piece. The color is deep chrome silver. The piece retains its original thick glass disk cemented into the smooth pontil scar underfoot. The double-walled and silvered glass top was blown in one piece, with an acorn shaped finial, and decorated with a leaf chain vine around the top. The cover retains its original thick glass disk cemented into the smooth pontil scar on the flat undersurface, and may or may not be original to the piece. If the pair is a marriage, the closure methods are the same, but there is a notable difference in the scale, style, and quality of the engraving. $950.00

Blown flint glass covered server, made in the United States circa 1855 – 1870, possibly in the Pennsylvania area or the greater Boston area in New England, and measuring 5¾" tall when covered. The wide flat bowl measures 5¾" in diameter. The top, made of blown glass and decorated in the "vintage" pattern, is a deep dome shape. Blown in one piece, the cover has a large ball finial handle, which has been ground flat on top to smooth the pontil scar. This covered piece was probably created for use as a cheese or fruit server or another food that could be piled into the dish, as specialty table items were a true Victorian fancy. The bowl has a flat rim, and retains its original cork seal covered with a beige paper seal over the rough pontil scar underfoot. The color is light chrome silver, and there are some minor cloudy patches and surface scratches underfoot, consistent with age. $650.00

Blown flint glass covered sugar bowl, made in the United States circa 1855 – 1870, probably at the Boston & Sandwich Glass Company or other Boston area maker, measuring 6¼" tall when covered, with both pieces engraved in a matching pattern consisting of grapes, flowers, leaves, vines, and curling tendrils. The cover has an applied onion-shaped finial handle, which is slightly crooked, a minor mishap that occurred in the annealing phase. The double-walled silvered glass bottom retains its original cork inserted in the rough pontil scar, with a reddish-black color circular seal intact over the seal. $800.00

Blown lead glass creamer, measuring 3¾" tall, made in Bohemia or Germany circa 1870 – 1890, with a formed spout, applied clear glass handle, and decorated in an intricate pattern consisting of birds, leaves, vines, and Gothic arches with the applied granulate crystal etching method. The interior is bright gold washed. The piece retains its original foil seal, covered with a round glass disc cemented into the smoothed pontil scar underfoot. $250.00

Pair of blown flint glass cream or syrup pitchers, made in the United States circa 1855 – 1870, with formed spouts, applied clear glass handles finished in the crimped and turned method, and measuring 6½" tall. The bulbous body and angled top rim forms resemble free-blown glass pitchers made in Pittsburgh, New Jersey, and New England in the earlier decades of the nineteenth century. The color is bright chrome silver. The pitchers have a cork inserted into rough pontil scars underfoot, which may not be original. $1,200.00 pair

Blown flint glass bowl, made in the United States circa 1855 – 1870, probably a Boston area, New England maker, measuring 3¼" tall with a 3¾" diameter, and wheel engraved with the "vintage" pattern. The color is bright chrome silver. The piece retains its original cork inserted into the rough pontil scar. $400.00

Pair of blown flint glass footed bowls, made in the United States circa 1855 – 1870, each measuring 5" tall, with a 4" open diameter, with a round, cup shape, marvered stem, and spread to a large, round foot. Both bowls retain their original cork seal, inserted into the rough pontil scar underfoot. The pieces are plain, without surface embellishment, and the color is bright silver mirror chrome. $850.00 pair

Blown lead glass egg holder or cup, made in Bohemia or Germany circa 1860 – 1880, maker unknown. The piece measures 2½" tall, has bright gold washed interior, and retains its original metal or heavy foil seal stamped with the letter "P," and covered with a glass disc cemented into the smooth pontil scar underfoot. $150.00

Blown flint glass cream pitcher, made in the United States circa 1855 – 1870, probably a Boston area New England maker, measuring 6" tall, with a bulbous shaped body, formed spout, angled and pulled rim, and applied, clear glass handle which was finished with a crimping instrument near the bottom attachment area. The piece is wheel engraved in a variant "vintage" large scale pattern consisting of widely spaced grapes, stylized blossoms and leaves, and curling tendrils all around the body. The piece has a marvered platform round foot. It retains its original cork seal inserted into the unpolished pontil scar underfoot. The piece is bright brilliant chrome silver with little evidence of wear. $1,200.00

Salts

Pair of blown flint glass footed master salt cellars, made in the United States circa 1855 – 1880, probably by a Boston area maker, measuring 2¼" tall, and 2" in diameter, engraved in an intricate and well-executed flower and leaf pattern encircling the outside of the bowls. Both pieces retain their original cork seals inserted into the unpolished pontil scars underfoot. $500.00

Rare blown cased cranberry glass cut to silvered footed master salt, made in the United States circa 1860 – 1880, probably by the New England Glass Company, and measuring 3¼" tall. The round cup-shaped bowl has cut circles around the top rim, and again along the rim of the foot. The cut design consists of interesting lines and flat cut ovals in a geometric pattern, which resembles the English cased glass made by Varnish and Thomson from a decade earlier. The piece has a tiny cork inserted into an unpolished pontil scar underfoot, which deviates from the normal closure methods perfected in England. $1,500.00

Blown uranium green lead glass footed master salt holder, made in England circa 1849 – 1855, measuring 2¾" tall, with a 2¾" open diameter and large scale rounded foot. The piece retains its original metal seal impressed "Hale Thomson's Patent London" covered with a circular glass disc cemented into the polished pontil scar underfoot. Unusual color later known as "vaseline glass." $1,600.00

Pair of blown lead glass footed master salt holders, made in England circa 1849 – 1855, each measuring 3¼" tall and 3" across the open diameter, with a gold interior that was probably achieved by an additional gather of colored glass through which the silvering gives a gold appearance, as opposed to chemical staining used in the Bohemian or German examples. There is a slight deviation between the size of the round foot in each piece, as well as a difference in the diameter of the pontil opening and closure seal. Each piece retains its original metal disc impressed "Varnish & Co. Patent London" covered by the circular glass seal cemented into place underfoot. $2,000.00 pair

Blown flint glass master salt holder, made in the United States circa 1855 – 1870, probably in New England, and wheel engraved in the "vintage" pattern around the outside surface. The salt has a collar foot, and retains its original cork seal inserted into the rough pontil scar underfoot. The color is bright silver mirror, and there is one small area of silvering loss underfoot. $250.00 pair

Matched pair of blown flint glass footed master salt holders, made in the United States circa 1855 – 1870 by the New England Glass Company, Cambridge, Massachusetts. Each piece measures 3¼" tall, with a round, cup shape and medium round foot. The salts are heavy for their size and retain the original metal discs stamped "NEG Co." covered with circular glass discs cemented into the polished pontil openings underfoot. The color is bright chrome silver, and there is some surface staining on the interior of each bowl consistent with the effect of moisture and salt. $800.00 pair

Pair of blown lead glass master salt holders, made in Bohemia circa 1860 – 1880, probably by the Hugo Wolf Company, Iglau, measuring 2½" tall and 2¾" across the top diameter, with a deep amber gold washed interior. Each piece retains its original metal seal, which reads "WH," covered by a glass disc. It is most likely, however, that these seals were inserted upside-down, in error, and therefore, if reversed, would correctly read "HW" for the Hugo Wolf Company, Bohemia. $1,200.00 pair

Blown lead glass master salt holder, made in Bohemia or Germany circa 1860 – 1880, measuring 2¾" tall, with a deep amber gold washed interior, and decorated in a surface wheel engraved "vintage" pattern. The piece retains its original metal disc and glass seal cemented into the smooth pontil scar underfoot. $300.00

Blown flint glass footed master salt holder, made in the United States circa 1855 – 1870, probably New England area maker, measuring 3" tall, and wheel engraved in horizontal "vintage" pattern. The color is bright mirror silver. The piece retains its original cork seal inserted into the small pontil scar underfoot. $325.00

Blown and molded non-flint glass footed master salt, made in Bohemia circa 1860 – 1880, measuring 2¼" tall, with a paneled or ribbed appearance achieved by mold-pressing the top portion of the piece, then switching the blowing tools, and holding the piece upright in order for the molded area to fall into the lower part. The result is that the "ribs" cannot be felt on the exterior surface of the bowl, although the visual illusion remains. There is a cork inserted into the pontil scar underfoot, not original to the piece, and the salt holder is very light in weight. $250.00

Blown flint glass footed master salt holder, made in the United States circa 1855 – 1870, measuring 2¾" tall, probably by New England Glass Company or another Boston area maker, and decorated with a finely executed wheel engraved design consisting of a large scale floral and leaf chain around the outside surface of the cup-shaped bowl. The color is dark chrome silver. The piece has a cork inserted into the polished pontil scar underfoot, which may not be original to the piece. There is some minor flaking of the silvering along the edge of the foot rim and underfoot. $195.00

Blown flint glass footed master salt holder, measuring 3" tall, made in the United States circa 1855 – 1870, probably Boston & Sandwich Glass Company, and wheel engraved with the word "Mother" enclosed in a well executed wreath consisting of flowers, leaves, and a bow. The piece is bright mirror silver in color. It retains its original cork inserted into the rough pontil scar underfoot, which is partially covered by a reddish-silver paper seal. $725.00

Blown flint glass footed master salt, measuring 3" tall, made in the United States circa 1855 – 1870, with a cup-shaped bowl, medium stem, and round foot, wheel engraved in the "vintage" pattern. The piece retains its original cork seal inserted into the sharp edged pontil scar underfoot. The color is bright mirror silver. $175.00

Large blown lead glass footed master salt, made in the United States circa 1855 – 1870, probably by the New England Glass Company, Cambridge, Massachusetts, measuring 3½" tall, and very heavy for its size. The bowl is cup shaped, and the surface is plain deep chrome silver in color, without any embellishment. The piece retains its original thick glass seal cemented into the polished pontil scar underfoot. $450.00

Blown flint glass master salt, made in the United States circa 1855 – 1870, probably New England area maker, possibly Boston & Sandwich Glass Company, measuring 3" tall, and custom engraved with the name "Myra" in old English script. There is a stylized leaf and vine garland underneath the name. The piece retains its original cork seal inserted into the small pontil scar underfoot, with remnants of a reddish-silver paper seal. $650.00

Blown lead glass footed master salt holder, made in England circa 1849 – 1855, measuring 2¾ tall, with a wide round bowl, pedestal stem, and round foot. The piece retains its original metal disc impressed "Thomson's Patent London" covered by a glass disc cemented into the smoothed pontil scar underfoot. $1,000.00

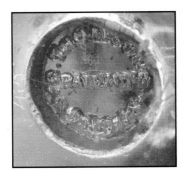

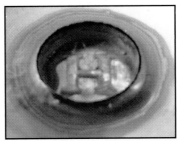

Blown lead glass master saltcellar, made in Bohemia circa 1860 – 1880, measuring 2¼" tall, with a bright amber gold washed interior. The piece retains its original metal disc seal impressed with the single letter "H," which may be attributable to the Hugo Wolf Company, Iglau. There is some hazing and cloudiness underfoot. $425.00

Blown flint glass footed individual saltcellar, made in the United States circa 1855 – 1870, measuring 2" tall, and decorated in the "vintage" pattern by wheel engraving. The piece has a thin layer of metal plating material over the bottom, with evidence of a slightly protruding cork. This was likely an additional measure to protect the original seal. $125.00

Blown flint glass master salt, made in the United States circa 1855 – 1870, New England Glass Company, Cambridge, Massachusetts, measuring 2¾" tall and with a 3" diameter across the top rim. The piece is dark chrome, and it retains its original metal seal stamped "NEG Co." covered with a glass disc, with the number 36 engraved on the surface of the disc as well as adjacent to the polished pontil hole. This would appear to indicate that the piece was smoothed, and a disc cut away possibly to allow silvering, then, re-matched to the original piece after the silver coating was achieved. $450.00

Large blown flint glass footed master salt holder, made in the United States circa 1855 – 1870, likely by the New England Glass Company, measuring 3" tall, with its original thick glass plug cemented into a polished pontil scar underfoot. The color is dark chrome, and there is some minor hazing evident along the top rim and on the foot. $200.00

Blown and molded non-flint glass footed master salt, made in Bohemia circa 1860 – 1880, measuring 2¾" tall, with a cup-shaped bowl, bright gold washed interior, and decorated in the "vintage" pattern by the applied crystal granulate application etching technique. The piece retains its original lead plug, but no glass disc. $275.00

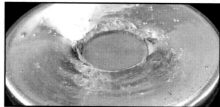

Blown lead glass footed individual salt, made in Bohemia circa 1860 – 1880, measuring 2" tall, with a bright amber gold washed interior, and retaining its original metal seal stamped with the single letter "H," presumably attributed to Hugo Wolf, Iglau. Use of the single letter may have been necessary because of the limitations imposed by the smaller size of the piece, although this is speculative. There is a glass disc covering the metal seal. $175.00

Pair of blown flint glass footed master salt holders, made in the United States circa 1855 – 1870, probably Boston & Sandwich Glass Company or other New England area maker, each measuring about 3" tall, with cup-shaped bowls, and wheel engraved in the "vintage" pattern. Both salt holders retain their original cork seals imbedded in the rough pontil scar underfoot. The color is bright silver mirror, and the pieces are heavy for their size. $600.00 pair

Pair of blown flint glass saltcellars, made in the United States circa 1855 – 1870, each measuring a little over 1½" tall, retaining their original cork seals imbedded into the rough pontil scar underfoot, with one showing remnants of a reddish-silver paper label on the bottom. There is some minor spotting and cloudiness underfoot to both salts. $125.00 pair

Blown flint glass footed individual saltcellar, made in the United States circa 1855 – 1870, probably by the New England Glass Company, measuring 1¾" tall, and retaining its original thick glass plug inserted into the polished pontil scar underfoot. $125.00

Blown and molded non-lead glass individual footed saltcellar, made in Bohemia or Germany circa 1860 – 1880, with a gold washed interior, and decorated with the "vintage" pattern in the applied granulate crystal etching technique. The piece retains its original metal wafer seal and glass disc cemented into the polished pontil scar underfoot. $95.00

Blown, rare cased and cut lead glass decanter with stopper, made in England circa 1849 – 1855, measuring 8" tall, with a swirled rib pattern, amethyst cut to silver, with the original metal seal impressed "Varnish & Co. Patent London" and glass disc cemented into the smooth pontil scar underfoot. The piece has an eight-sided paneled neck, pear-shaped base, and simulated rope turn cut foot rim. The stopper has a turban shape and cut swirled rib pattern to match. This large decanter was originally thought to be a perfume or cologne holder, however, its sheer size and weight would make its use for m'lady seem rather unlikely. There is one area above the elongated stopper insert that has minor case glass flaking. $4,000.00

Candlesticks, or "kerzenleuchters" in German, were made in varying heights, shapes, and sizes, and with a variety of additional decorative embellishments, including painting, applied crushed crystal granulate etching, wheel engraving, and hand painting. While American examples were subject to the same wheel engraving as tableware, including the typical "vintage" pattern, the English-made colored and cased cut to silver pieces with the same technique applied to other forms.

Silvered glass gazing globes are spheres on foot, and were made in England from at least 1840. An excerpt from one description of the 1851 Crystal Palace Exhibition indicates the public's familiarity with silvered glass globes. In the United States, several patents were granted in the manufacture of silvered glass globes, including patent number 70,325 registered to Edward Dithridge of Pittsburgh, Pennsylvania, in October 1867. Dithridge's method involved the creation of two separate pieces of blown, double-walled glass, which were subjugated to silvering and then joined to create the globe on stand.

The New England Glass Company, which was one of the most prolific makers of silvered glass, produced gazing globes in many different heights and sizes. An illustration from the *Ballou's Pictorial Drawing Room Companion*, 1855, shows the interior of the New England Glass showroom where silvered glass globes can easily be recognized. The New England Glass footed gazing globes were blown in one piece, probably with the use of a mold to insure perfect shaping of the round top. Globes were made in a great variety of sizes, and were used to enhance and reflect the light fueled by oil, gas, or kerosene lamps or candlelight.

There is much speculation about the use of these globes, and one of the most common, although a misnomer, is the idea that these globes were made as wig-stands. Wigs were more common in the eighteenth century, far earlier than the production of silvered glass globes, and the size of the average silvered glass globe was simply too large to accommodate a wig.

Another legend, perhaps more plausible, is that the globes, placed strategically on the banquet table, could be viewed by servants to allow a view of the dining guests so as to allow a visual cue when a glass needed a refill or a course needed to be removed. A similar belief is that these globes were placed at the head of the table, near the master of the household, who could then use a discreet gesture to summon the butler. The term "butler's ball" was based on that theory.

These speculations, no matter how romantic, cannot be proven, but the globe on foot is fairly unique to silvered glass, and was probably assigned to other clever uses throughout the period of production.

United States Patent Office.

EDWARD DITHRIDGE, OF PITTSBURG, PENNSYLVANIA.

Letters Patent No. 70,325, dated October 29, 1867.

IMPROVED PROCESS OF MANUFACTURING SILVERED GLASSWARE.

The Schedule referred to in these Letters Patent and making part of the same.

TO ALL WHOM IT MAY CONCERN:

Be it known that I, EDWARD DITHRIDGE, of Pittsburg, in the county of Allegheny, and State of Pennsylvania, have invented certain new and useful improvements in the Process for Manufacturing Silvered Glassware; and do hereby declare that the following is a full, clear, and exact description thereof, reference being had to the accompanying drawings, and to the letters of reference marked thereon, which form a part of this specification, in which—

Figure 1 is an elevation, with the globe and holder or stand placed in proper relation to each other, and Figure 2 is a similar view of the holder.

The nature of my invention consists in an improved method of manufacturing glassware to be silvered, whereby the cement is prevented from coming in contact with the silver, substantially as hereinafter set forth.

A represents the stand, which should be made longer than required. It is then reheated and doubled in, so as to form a recess or receptacle for the cement, as fully seen in the drawings. A hole is left in the bottom of the stand for the introduction of the silver. In larger articles this receptacle is formed somewhat differently. A piece of molten glass is gathered on the end of the blowing pipe, and placed on the end of the article in which it is desired to produce the double part; it is then sucked in, and the cavity fashioned with the ordinary glass-blowers' tools. B represents a globe, provided with a tubular projection, e, through which the silver is inserted. In joining the globe and stand together, place the projection e in the recess in stand A, and fill the cavity with cement. Thus it will be observed that the difficulty hitherto experienced in connecting two or more parts of silvered glassware is entirely obviated by a very simple process, as it is impossible for the cement to come in contact with the silver, and thus mar the finish of the article.

Having thus fully described my invention, what I claim, and desire to secure by Letters Patent, is—

Providing a recess for the reception of tenons, so as to form any article of silvered glassware composed of any number of pieces, without bringing the cement used in contact with the silver on the glass, substantially as set forth and described.

In testimony that I claim the foregoing as my own I affix my signature in presence of two witnesses

EDWD. DITHRIDGE.

Witnesses:
Jos. A. Butler,
E. D. Dithridge.

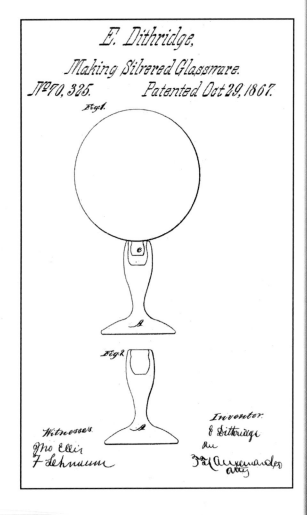

Showroom of the New England Glass Company from *Ballou's Pictorial Drawing Room Companion*, January 20, 1855. Author's collection.

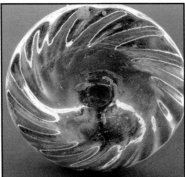

Blown and molded non-lead glass tall candlestick holder, made in Bohemia circa 1870 – 1890, measuring 9½" tall, with a swirled rib effect achieved by partial molding and marvering, with a rimmed cup, baluster stem, and graduated step pedestal foot. The piece has remnants of painted white rings, and retains its original silver paper seal with glass disc over the pontil scar under the concave foot. $450.00

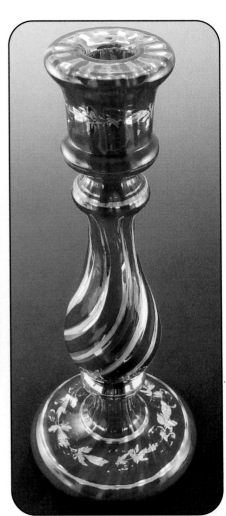

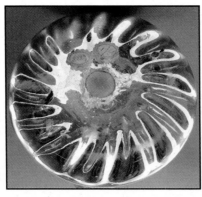

Blown and molded non-lead glass tall candlestick holder, made in Bohemia circa 1860 – 1880, measuring 11" tall with a swirled rib effect, and with bright red flashing cut to silver, accented with white cold enamel paint stripes. The cup and foot are cut from red to silver in a leaf and chain pattern with additional white accents. This method of mock casing was likely made to replicate the true double-glass layer cased silvered glass pieces made in England as evidenced by the similarity in overt appearance. The stem is a baluster shape with a molded knop and round, ribbed foot. The piece retains its original metal wafer seal and glass disc, and there are two old paper labels, which show ink markings that are not discernable. $1,200.00

Blown and molded lead glass taper holder, made in Bohemia circa 1860 – 1880, measuring 7½" tall, with an intricate applied crystal granulate etched design consisting of leaves and curling tendrils, together with a simple horizontal leaf chain around the cup. The inner cup candle holder is bright amber gold washed. The piece retains its original metal wafer seal and glass disc cemented into the smoothed pontil scar underfoot. $395.00

Blown and molded non-lead glass candlestick, made in Bohemia circa 1870 – 1890, measuring 8½" tall, in the swirled rib pattern achieved by partial molding and marvering. The piece has a columnar stem and graduated platform foot, and has a cork imbedded into the rough pontil scar underfoot, which is not original. There is some haze spottiness on the upper surface of the foot, as well as blotch silvering loss to the upper cup and rim. $250.00

Blown and molded non-flint glass tall candlestick, made in Bohemia or Germany circa 1860 – 1890, measuring 12" tall, with a baluster stem and large, round foot. There are two white painted rings around the candle cup and no further embellishment. This may likely be a case where the original painting was lost, since most similar shaped pieces of this stature have other painted areas. The piece retains its original metal seal and glass disc underfoot. There is mottled hazy cloudiness on the upper surface of the foot, as well as patchy thinning of the silver and on the stem. $450.00

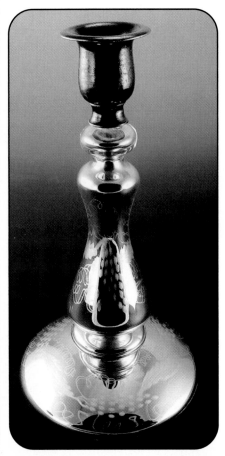

Blown molded flint glass tall candle holder, made in the United States circa 1860 – 1880, measuring 9½" tall, with a gray metal cup affixed to the glass. The piece was likely made at the New England Glass Company or the Boston Silver Glass Company. The candlestick is engraved in a fine scale "vintage" pattern and the color is bright chrome mirror silver. In this case, the silvering was likely introduced through the top of the piece, which was then sealed and covered with the metal cap. There is a smoothed pontil scar under the large, concave foot and the piece is very heavy for its size. $1,400.00

Blown and molded lead glass candleholder, made in Bohemia circa 1860 – 1880, measuring 7½" tall, with a round rimmed candle cup, molded pillar stem, and decorated in an intricate "vintage" pattern with the applied crystal granulate etching technique. The piece is bright mirror silver in color, and retains its original light metal wafer seal and glass disc cemented into the polished pontil scar underfoot. $350.00

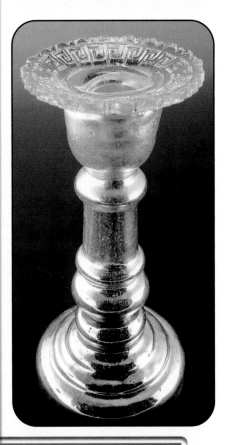

Blown and molded soda lime glass candleholder, made in Germany or Bohemia circa 1870 – 1890, measuring 7½" tall, with an unusual pressed glass bobeche in the Greek Key pattern attached to the top rim. The piece has a tapered cylindrical shape with graduated sized knops, and a round foot, and a cork imbedded in the rough pontil scar, which is not original. The silvering has been exposed to the atmosphere, and is faded and lightened with a bubbly patina. $175.00

Pair of blown and molded pink glass candleholders, in a ball shape, made in Czechoslovakia circa 1918 – 1930, each measuring 2¾" tall, and bearing their original circular foil label "Czecho-Slovakia" over the bottom. There is some minor cloudiness underfoot. $175.00

A rare pair of blown and molded flint glass gazing or banquet globes on foot, made in the United States circa 1870, and made according to the Edward Dithridge patent. Each measuring 10½" tall, the sphere-shaped globe was blown separately and joined to the stem. The circumference of the ball globe is 19", and the reverse baluster stem is medium length, with a narrow bottom then spread to a round foot measuring 4½" in diameter. The color is bright mirror chrome silver. Each stand retains its original cork seal imbedded into the rough pontil scar underfoot. $2,100.00

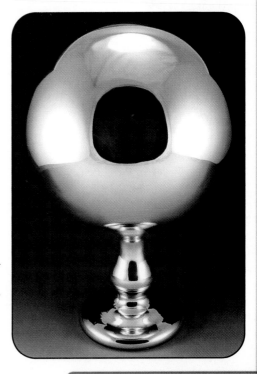

Blown molded flint glass gazing globe, made in the United States circa 1855 – 1870, New England Glass Company, Cambridge, Massachusetts, and measuring 12" tall with a 25" globe circumference. The piece was made in one contiguous piece, with a baluster stem and round foot. The color is bright mirror chrome silver. It retains its original cork seal imbedded into the unpolished pontil scar underfoot. $1,600.00

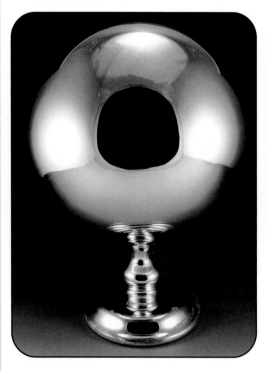

Blown molded flint glass gazing or globe, made in the United States circa 1855 – 1870, New England Glass Company, Cambridge, Massachusetts, and measuring 12" tall with a 28" globe circumference. The piece was made in one piece, with a platform balustroid stem and a round, plateau foot measuring 5½" in diameter. The color is dark chrome mirror. The piece retains its original cork seal imbedded into an unpolished pontil scar underfoot. There is some cloudiness and flake loss to the silvering around the edge and underneath the foot rim. $1,200.00

Blown and molded flint glass gazing or banquet globe on foot, made in the United States circa 1870, Pennsylvania, and according to the Dithridge patent outline. The globe and stand were made separately, and joined together. The piece measures 14" tall with a 28" circumference. The color is dark mirror chrome silver. There is a cork seal imbedded into the rough pontil scar underfoot, which appears to be original. There is some minor haze to the outer foot rim surface and underfoot. $1,500.00

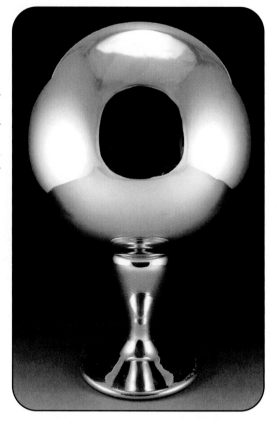

Blown and molded flint glass table globe, made in the United States circa 1855 – 1870, New England Glass Company, Cambridge, Massachusetts, measuring 9½" tall with a 19½" circumference. The piece was made in one piece. It retains its original cork seal imbedded into a rough pontil scar underfoot, with remnants of a beige paper label. The color is bright chrome mirror silver, and there is some haziness on the lower portion of the stem and on the top surface of the round foot. $1,000.00

Figures, Match Holders, Paperweights, and Specialty Items

Molded figures, depicting Christ, the Mother Mary, or Christian saints, were made in Bohemia from the mid-nineteenth century, and were used for shrines or worship in the home.

After the turn of the century and before World War II, thin and featherweight animal figures were produced in Germany and exported to the United States to be sold as novelties. The stag or deer figure was the most popular, and examples have survived in spite of their fragility.

Match holders with rough granulate strike surfaces were made in Bohemia and Germany. While this shape is sometimes confused with a toothpick holder, the inclusion of a strike area offers no other interpretation.

Paperweights were made in England and the United States, and decorated with cased cutting, wheel engraving, or sometimes, left plain. Intricate cut and cased silvered glass knobs and tiebacks were made, and several pair are illustrated in this chapter.

Finally, truly utilitarian wares were represented in silvered mercury glass. The curtain tieback, or curtain pin holder, was made in the United States, while the cut, cased, and faceted cabinet knobs, as well as the cased and cut tiebacks, could have been in France.

Blown molded non-flint glass figure, thought to be Saint Ann, made in Bohemia circa 1865 – 1880, measuring 6¼" tall, with the initials "J J. C" for the Joseph Janke Company, and retaining its original paper seal underfoot. The piece is plain light mirror silver, and there is some minor haze near the bottom rim. $300.00

Pair of blown and molded non-flint glass figural elephants, made circa 1900 – 1930, with applied glass eyes, the larger measuring 4¼" in length and 3" tall, the smaller measuring 2½" long. Each piece has been silvered through the trunk and the ears, tails, and legs are finished in an opaque lime green. These whimsical animals resemble Italian examples, but are clearly German made, as an oval paper label in gold and black is printed "Made in Germany." $175.00 the pair.

Pair of blown and molded non-flint glass figural deer or stags, made circa 1900 – 1930, with applied glass eyes, ears, and antlers, and silvered through the formed mouth. The large figure measures 4½" long and stands 4½" tall, the smaller measures 3½" long and 3¾" tall. Both figures have clear glass stands attached to the bottom of the four legs, and the large figure has a "Made in Germany" label, which appears to be original. There is no damage to the glass, and the silvering is blotchy and spotty near the open mouth, down the front chest and the lower legs of both figures. $225.00 the pair

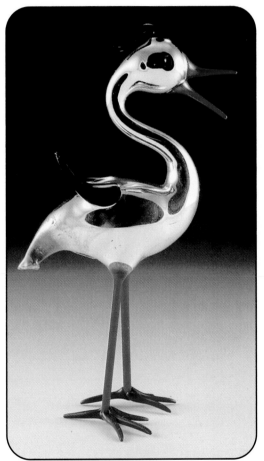

Blown and shaped non-flint glass figural crane, made circa 1900 – 1930, with applied glass eyes and a red beak and legs, black wings and head feather, measuring 6" tall, with original paper label "Made in Germany." The silvering was introduced through the hind tail area, which is open. There is some haziness and patch loss to the neck and body. $125.00

Blown and molded non-flint glass footed wooden match holder with strike area, made in Bohemia circa 1870 – 1890, measuring 3½" tall, with an applied crystal granulate etched "vintage" pattern around the bright amber gold washed cup projecting from a round plateau foot. The piece has a ½" wide band around the raised foot, which has been embellished with a gritty substance similar to sandpaper used to strike the matches to flame. The match holder has its original metal wafer seal and glass disc cemented into the rough pontil scar underfoot, and has cloudiness and loss of silvering to the foot beneath the strike area. $125.00

Blown and molded non-lead glass match holder, made in Bohemia or Germany circa 1870 – 1890, measuring 3" tall, with a cylindrical shape, bright amber gold washed interior cup, and decorated in the "vintage" pattern by the applied crystal granulate etch technique. The piece has a narrow band treated with a gritty application to serve as a striking area, and retains its original metal seal and glass disc cemented into the rough pontil scar underfoot. There is minor silvering loss to the top rim. $95.00

Blown and molded non-flint glass footed match holder, made in Bohemia circa 1870 – 1890, measuring 3¾" tall, and decorated with an intricate leaf and vine pattern with the applied crystal granulate etching technique. The piece has a bright gold washed cup, and a broad ¾" strike area on the surface of the round foot, and retains its original metal wafer seal and glass disc cemented into the rough pontil scar underfoot. There is blotchy patch loss of the silvering on the rim edge and underfoot. $125.00

Blown and molded non-lead glass footed match holder, made in Bohemia circa 1870 – 1890, measuring 3¾" tall, with a large, slightly concave plateau foot with a 1¼" broad strike area treated with a gritty substance. The piece is decorated with a "vintage" pattern around the gold washed cup, and retains its original metal seal and glass disc cemented into the unpolished pontil scar underfoot. There is some spot loss of silvering underfoot. $135.00

Blown flint glass paper-weight, made in the United States circa 1860 – 1880, probably New England Glass Company or Boston & Sandwich Glass Company, measuring 3½" in diameter and wheel engraved in a fine floral, fern, and leaf pattern across the top surface. The piece retains its original round glass plug cemented into the polished pontil scar underneath. $350.00

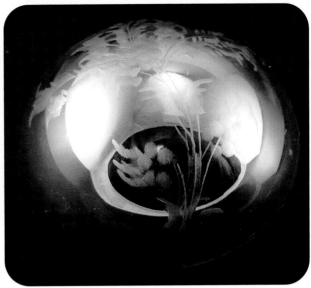

Blown and molded paperweight, made in the United States circa 1860 – 1880, probably Boston & Sandwich Glass Company, wheel engraved with the initials "M. L. D." in old English script, with a flower and leaf swag above and below the initials. The piece has deep cut oval panels around the edges, and measures 2¾" in diameter. There is a silvered center cell within the thick, clear glass weight, which has been sealed with a glass disc. $325.00

Pair of cased blue lead glass cut to silvered curtain tie-backs, made in the United States circa 1860 – 1880, New England Glass Company or Boston & Sandwich Glass Company, each measuring 2¼" diameter and 3½" long, with silver-plated shanks, and original threaded screw nails. The cased blue layer has a 12-point star cut into the center, and ovals around the rim, and the back has been cut with elongated oval panels. Unmarked. $550.00

Pair of cased cranberry lead glass cut to silvered knobs, the glass possibly made in the United States, maker unknown, with brass fittings, measuring 2¼" in diameter and 2¾" long. Both pieces marked Made in France on the distal surface of the brass area. The cased cranberry pink glass layer has a 12-point star cut into the center flat surface of the knob and ovals around the rim. There are elongated oval panels on the back. It is possible that the glass knobs were made in the United States, and the brass fittings were imported and then attached to the glass at some point in manufacture. There is no documentation available to provide further information about silvered glass made in France, and the style of casing and cutting could be English or American. $600.00

Blown and molded flint glass curtain tie-back, made in the United States circa 1855 – 1880, measuring 4½" long with a 2¾" diameter, engraved in the "vintage" pattern. The shank and threaded screw portion are made of gray metal, similar to pewter or Britannia, which has been cemented to the silvered glass front. $150.00

Caring for Silvered Mercury Glass

Although glass is impervious to most environmental damage, the silvered layer within each piece can deteriorate when exposed to air. Patch loss, flaking, cloudiness, and darkening of the silvered coating will reduce the relative value of the piece. Since the survival of the seal is extremely important, the cardinal rule regarding care and cleaning is never to submerge a piece of silvered mercury glass in a water bath or allow water or vapor to come in contact with the seal on bottom. Most of the sealing methods for silvered mercury glass include glue or cement, which will loosen easily if allowed to become wet. Even a simple cork seal can become loosened if wet, so it is better to completely avoid the thought of a water bath. Even when following the suggested cleaning techniques, extra care must be taken to avoid getting any type of solution around the pontil scar or opening. If the piece does *not* have any type of seal, a simple piece of tape placed carefully over the hole should protect the interior. Remember that solutions used will run down to the foot, so a sponge or other implement must be used at all times rather than spraying the item directly. This is extremely important.

Many of the surface decorations can become worn or soiled. It is recommended that prior to cleaning the surface of any silvered mercury glass item, a careful assessment about the type of applied decoration must be performed. Improper cleaning will result in the loss of decoration, so it is important to understand how the piece was decorated.

Although the methods outlined in the following paragraphs have been successful, the author will not be held responsible for any damage incurred while attempting to clean mercury glass. If you are in doubt, contact a local museum or professional restorer about alternative methods.

With the caveat clearly stated, there are, however, techniques for cleaning mercury glass that have had excellent results.

A plain mercury glass item without any additional surface embellishment may be cleaned as follows: Spread a cloth towel on a flat work surface and place the piece on the towel.

Using a pad made with several folded or bunched sheets of paper toweling and an ordinary glass cleaning solution, spray a small amount directly onto the paper toweling, but never on the glass itself. Carefully wipe the surface lightly to remove soil, fingerprints, and dust, and polish with a dry paper towel. This simple cleaning method can often restore the surface silvery brilliance to glass that has been subject to years of neglect.

For engraved pieces and mercury glass items decorated in the crystal granulate etched technique (the surface decorations are gritty to the touch, and often discolored when found) as in the small illustrated beaker shown on page 156, you may try the following method using a cotton swab in a remote area first to insure that the cleaning will not cause damage to the decoration:

On a padded work surface as above, place the piece to be cleaned. Using rubber gloves, take a small amount of commercial automatic dish detergent liquid onto a sponge (the type used in electric dishwashers) and lightly dab the surface areas to be cleaned. The bleach in the solution will whiten areas made brown, gray, or even black by accumulated dust and grime. You can use repeated circular motions and turn the sponge over as the soil is removed. Rinse the sponge thoroughly and wipe the dishwashing solution away from the glass surface, repeating the step until the glass is clear. To neutralize the bleach in the solution, and to remove the "slippery" residue, you may use ordinary table vinegar on a fresh sponge and wipe the surface again.

Repeat with a rinsed sponge to remove the vinegar, and dry carefully with a non-lint linen towel or paper towel. Avoid the impulse to rinse the piece under a running water faucet, as even tiny droplets of water can invade the seal underfoot.

If the surface is decorated with cold enamel paint, which is generally found on a satin matte ground, a very light, quick-touch sponging with a weak one-part dish detergent (not the electric diswasher type) and one-part lukewarm water solution, may remove surface soil. Make sure to sponge rinse the piece with water, repeating until the surface is clear of soap, and dry with light patting only. Do not use vinegar as the acid may damage or discolor the paint.

If the painting on the piece looks transparent or is found on a plain mirror surface, any attempts to clean the decoration will probably result in loss. In the early days of collecting this glass, mistakes in cleaning resulted in the total elimination of design.

Caring for any antique glass requires attention to task while cleaning, and fragile items must be protected from breakage. After the initial cleaning as described, an occasional dusting with a damp paper towel is all that is necessary to keep the silvered mercury glass looking brilliant.

Before cleaning.

After cleaning.

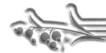

Mercury silvered glass is being reproduced in many countries. Dept. 56 and other contemporary collectible manufactures have created new pieces, often marketing them as mercury glass. New ornaments are plentiful, but globular candleholders and large handles vessels were made in Mexico from the 1970s and other items continue to be produced today.

The following group of items are contemporary and not to be confused with the authentic antique glass illustrated in the previous chapters. The red glass hurricane lamp on a mercury glass base has also been seen in other colors, such as blue and green. The bottom of the base is smooth, without the familiar pontil scar to indicate the piece was blown. The compote on foot and bowl have a clear glass disc glued underfoot, and have plastic and paper labels indicating Continental production.

Although not illustrated here, there have been large, double-handled vessels imported from Mexico in the last

10 – 20 years. Generally, these pieces are one-layered and have a ribbed effect. The naïve or unscrupulous may sell these new items as old, but the contemporary items are easily detectable by looking for clues to indicate sealing method, wear marks, and decorations. The color of the new mercury glass is also much brighter white silver, which looks very different than the chrome hues of authentic antique silvered mercury glass.

Recommended Museums

American Silvered Mercury Glass

Bennington Museum, Bennington, Vermont

Corning Glass Museum, Corning, New York

The Museum of American Glass, Wheaton Village, Millville, New Jersey

English Silvered Glass

Broadfield House Glass Museum, England

The Victoria & Albert Museum, London, England

Bohemian, English & American Mercury Glass

The New Orleans Museum of Art, New Orleans, Louisiana
(Harold Newman Collection)

Bibliography

Books:

Chipman, Frank. *The Romance of Old Sandwich Glass*. Sandwich Publishing Company, 1932.

Daniel, Dorothy. *Cut and Engraved Glass 1771 – 1905*. New York: Barrows & Company, 1950.

Dreppard, Carl W. *ABC's of Old Glass*. New York: Doubleday & Company, 1968.

Endres, Werner. *Silberglass: Bauernsilber: Formen, Techniuk, und Geschichte*. Munich, Germany: Callwey, 1983.

Hajdamach, Charles R. *British Glass 1800 – 1914*. England: Antique Collector's Club, 1991.

Hotchkiss, John F. *Art Glass Handbook with Prices*. 4th Edition. New York: Hawthorne Books, 1972.

Hughes, G. Bernard. *English Glass for the Collector 1660 – 1860*. New York: Preager Publishers, 1968.

Kovel, Ralph and Terry. *Know Your Antiques*. New York: Crown Publishing, 1967.

McKearnin, Helen and George. *Two Hundred Years of American Blown Glass*. New York: Crown Publishing, 1949.

McKearnin, Helen and George. *American Glass*. New York: Crown Publishing, 1941.

Moore, N. Hudson. *Old Glass European and American*. New York: Tudor Publishing Company, 1946.

Morris, Barbara. *Victorian Table Glass and Ornaments*. Barrie and Jenkins, 1978.

Newman, Harold. *An Illustrated Dictionary of Glass*. London: Thames and Hudson, 1977.

Papert, Emma. *The Illustrated Guide to American Glass*. New York: Hawthorn Books, Inc. 1972.

Revi, Albert Christian. *Nineteenth Century Glass: It's Genesis and Development*. Revised Edition. New York: Galahad Books, 1959, 1967.

Shuman, John A. III. *American Art Glass*. Paducah, Kentucky: Collector Books, 1988.

Watkins, Lura Woodside. *Cambridge Glass 1818 to 1888*. New York: Bramhall House, 1930.

Wilson, Kenneth M. *New England Glass and Glassmaking*. New York: Thomas Crowell Company, 1972.

Catalogs and other Published Materials:

Taylor, Gay LeCleire. "Mirrored Images: American Silvered Glass." Museum of American Glass, Millville, New Jersey. 2001.

———. "Gillender Glass: Story of a Company," Museum of American Glass, Millville, New Jersey, 1994.

Bishop, Barbara J. "The Rebirth of Carl Mattoni, Sandwich's Bohemian Glass Engraver." *The Acorn – Journal* of The Sandwich Glass Museum, Volume 7, 1997.

Christies East Auction Catalog: Nineteenth Century Furniture and Decorative Arts. New York, October 14, 1999.

Ferland, Donald. "Elegant Simplicity as Created by Louis Friederich Vaupel, Master Copper-Wheel Engraver," The Acorn, Journal of the Sandwich Glass Museum, Volume VI, 1995/96 pp91–116.

Lytwyn, Diane. "Silvered Glass Gazing Globes," *Antiques Journal*, July, 2000 pp 96–97.

Maycock, Susan E. "Louis Vaupel: His Life and Work at the New England Glass Company, *The Acorn*, Journal of the Sandwich Glass Museum, Volume VI 1995/96 pp 2–21.

Nelson, Kirk J. "A Century of Sandwich Glass," From the Collections of The Sandwich Glass Museum, Published by Patriot Press for The Sandwich Glass Museum, 1992.

Newman, Harold. "All That Glitters," Catalog from the New Orleans Museum. Published for the New Orleans Museum of Art.

Palais Kinsky Auctions. March 20, 2002. Vienna, Austria.

Richard Bourne Co., Inc. Auction Catalog; Early American Glass, October 23, 1984.

Spillman, Jane Shadel. "American Glass in the Bohemian Style," *Antiques Magazine*, January, 1996 pp 146–155.

Watkins, Lura Woodside. "American Silvered Glass," *Antiques Magazine*, October, 1942 pp 183–186

———. "Silver Glass," *The Glass Club Bulletin*, National Early American Glass Club, Boston, Massachusetts, Number 10, October, 1941.

Wilson, Kenneth M. "Collecting Glass and Knowledge Search and Research," *The Glass Club Bulletin of the National Early American Glass Club*, No. 137, Spring/Summer 1982. pp 3–6.

Index